Apocalypse

A Commentary on Revelation in Words and Images

Robert H. Smith

Illustrations by Albrecht Dürer

A Liturgical Press Book

THE LITURGICAL PRESS   Collegeville, Minnesota

Design by David Manahan, O.S.B.

Printed in the United States of America.

1 2 3 4 5 6 7 8

Library of Congress Cataloging-in-Publication Data

Smith, Robert H., 1932–
 Apocalypse : a commentary on Revelation in words and images / Robert H. Smith ; illustrations by Albrecht Dürer.
  p.   cm.
 Includes bibliographical references and index.
 ISBN 0-8146-2707-2 (alk. paper)
 1. Bible. N.T. Revelation—Commentaries. I. Title.

BS2825.3 .S58 2000
228'.077—dc21   00-026307

Contents

Acknowledgments

A number of people assisted in the writing of this book, even though they may have been unaware of it.

I owe a special debt to Basil Tsakonas, professor of New Testament and dean of the school of theology of the University of Athens (Greece) until his untimely death in 1995. He was a wonderful friend and facilitated my first extended stay on Patmos. On the island, the Greek Orthodox monks of the Monastery of St. John the Theologian have been unfailing in hospitality. In particular I think of the kindness of the monks Panteleimon, Symeon (guide and interpreter), and Chrysostomos (librarian and custodian of the monastery's collection of manuscripts).

Others on Patmos whom I must mention for the warmth of their welcome include Matthaios Melianos (director of the Patmian Theological School and since 1998 also mayor of Patmos) and his wife Anastasia, Maria and Vasili Karantanis, Stratos and Christina Kephalos, and Giorgos Kavouras.

From the beginning of this project, my wife Donna Duensing has accompanied me on journeys spiritual as well as geographical, and she has been the most constant voice of encouragement.

To all these, and to others who gave assistance but are not named here, I am grateful.

Notes

I had hoped to avoid footnotes altogether, but it may be useful to offer notes on these matters: 1) on the artist Albrecht Dürer, 2) on the way I categorize approaches to the book of Revelation, and 3) on the issue of church and culture.

Albrecht Dürer (1471–1528)

Dürer first produced his *Apocalypse* in 1498 and published a new edition in 1511 with one fresh woodcut (the small prefatory cut of John offering his work to the Virgin Mary and the Child). Dürer's *Apocalypse* was a big book, and his woodcuts were large, full-page illustrations, measuring approximately 11 x 15 inches. Woodcuts were at that time a German specialty and were intended for wide circulation among the general population. More expensive copper engravings and oil paintings were designed for wealthy merchants, princes, and patrons. Another piece of evidence regarding Dürer's view of his readership is the fact that his book contained the text of Revelation not only in Latin but also in German, since he wanted his book to be read not by clergy and the educated alone but by ordinary folk as well.

Dürer's godfather, Anton Koberger, published the Nuremberg Bible in 1483. In his own book of 1498, Dürer used the German translation of the Nuremberg Bible along with Latin text of the Vulgate. Dürer obviously knew not only the German translation of the Nuremberg Bible but also the eight woodcuts it carried on the book of Revelation. (All of them had previously appeared in the Cologne Bible of 1480.)

In two books printed a year apart, Kenneth Strand published Dürer's woodcuts on the Apocalypse along with the woodcuts produced by twelve other artists, some of whom were Dürer's predecessors and most of whom followed him. Strand's books show very clearly how innovative Dürer was while still honoring the tradition, and they show graphically how every woodcut artist of the sixteenth century was deeply indebted to Dürer. Kenneth Strand, *Woodcuts to the Apocalypse in Dürer's Time* (Ann Arbor Publishers, 1968) and *Woodcuts to the Apocalypse from the Early 16ᵗʰ Century* (Ann Arbor Publishers, 1969).

On the history of the illustration of the book of Revelation, see M. R. James, *The Apocalypse in Art* (Oxford University Press, 1931) and especially Frederick van der Meer, *Apocalypse: Visions from the Book of Revelation in Western Art* (New York: Alpine Fine Arts Collection, 1978). M. R. James writes that Dürer "dominated" all but a few of the illustrators who came after him, while van der Meer, paraphrasing Emil Male, says that Dürer took hold of the Apocalypse as Dante did of hell.

Splendid biographies of Dürer have been published by Erwin Panofsky (*The Life and Art of Albrecht Dürer,* Princeton 1955) and Jane Campbell Hutchison (*Albrecht Dürer: A Biography,* Princeton 1990).

Fundamentalist, Mainline, and Liberationist Readings

Admittedly the terms "fundamentalist," "mainline," and "liberationist" oversimplify the complexity of contemporary Christian viewpoints. Nevertheless, as rough as these categories and labels may be, I have found them helpful as I have tried to organize my thinking about approaches to the book of Revelation. The easiest way for me to communicate what I mean by these terms is not to offer another definition of each viewpoint, adding to what I say in the text, but to name authors and works I think of as representatives of each approach. Writers in any one category do not agree with one another on every point of interpretation, but they do tend to agree with others in the same category concerning the basic approach they take to the book of Revelation and its relevance for teaching and living today.

Under the label "fundamentalism" I have in mind the approach which is called, more technically speaking, "premillennial dispensationalism." It features ideas which may sound foreign to Christians in mainline denominations, ideas like the rapture, the future seven-year tribulation, the conversion of 144,000 Israelites who will work as missionaries during the tribulation period, the rise of a ten-nation successor to the ancient Roman Empire, the coming battle of Armageddon to be followed by a literal thousand-year kingdom of peace on earth, the final rebellion, and the Great White Throne judgment. Instead of speaking of "premills" or "dispensationalists," I use the term "fundamentalist," since this term is well known and the approach in view is held in some fashion by practically all fundamentalists.

The notion of a rapture at the time of a secret second coming of Christ to catch up faithful Christians to heaven and the integration of the rapture into a premillennial dispensationalist scheme are the work of John Nelson Darby (1800–1882). His ideas were eagerly received by Cyrus Scofield (1843–1921), who cast them into the form they have enjoyed ever since. The scheme eventually achieved nearly canonical status by means of the notes in the Scofield Reference Bible, first published in 1909 (revised in 1917) and republished many times since.

This approach has been championed by Dallas Theological Seminary and disseminated in the writings of its past president John Walvoord and popularized by Hal Lindsey, one of its best known graduates. Walvoord wrote a commentary on Revelation (1966) and a book called *Armageddon, Oil, and the Middle East Crisis* (rev. ed. 1990). Hal Lindsey is best known for his book *The Late Great Planet Earth* (1970), which sold as many as thirty million copies. Jack Van Impe and others spread the gospel of dispensationalism via their radio and television broadcasts. Tim LaHaye, besides writing a commentary on Revelation (1973), has written with Jerry B. Jenkins a series of novels which are fictionalized versions of the premill dispensationalist scheme. *Left Behind*, the first volume in the series (1995), opens with an account of the rapture. A seventh volume in the series is announced for publication in 2000.

I use "mainline" to cover a very large territory. In it I include a broad spectrum of people from evangelicals (itself a broad category) to liberals. One thing these Christians have in common is that they are not dispensationalists. They write of the future in terms of the scheme presented in the classical creeds. The Apostles' Creed and the Nicene Creed speak with great reserve of the future coming of Christ as judge of the living and the dead, of the resurrection of the body, and of the life everlasting or the life of the world to come. Evangelicals understand these matters more literally, while others insist on uncertainty concerning the details of the future, and the more liberal maintain that these items in the creeds must be understood figuratively or symbolically.

The following writers of commentaries on Revelation seem to me to fit into this broad category: David Aune (3 vol. 1997–1998), G. Beasley-Murray (1978), M. Eugene Boring (1989), G. B. Caird (1966), Charles Giblin (1991), Wilfrid Harrington (1993), Richard Jeske (1983), Gerhard Krodel (1989), Robert Mounce (2nd ed. 1998), J. Roloff (1993), J. P. M. Sweet (1979), C. H. Talbert (1994), and Adela Yarbro Collins (1979).

"Liberationist" is my third category. Liberals in mainline denominations have become increasingly receptive to the concerns raised by liberationists, so the boundary between liberals and liberationists is at times fuzzy. And, of course, liberationists are by no means all alike. One thing liberationists share, however, is a critical view of any theology which reduces God's sphere of influence to the inner life of the individual soul. Liberationists reject that reductionism and stress that the soul or spirit always and only has its life within the context of the body, and every body lives in a particular historical place. All theological thinking is influenced by its particular social, economic, and political context and in turn seeks to address that context.

When I speak of liberationist interpretation of Revelation, I have in mind commentaries written by the following: Allan Boesak (1987), Pablo Richard (1995), and Christopher Rowland (1993). Richard Bauckham belongs here with his books *The Climax of Prophecy* (1992) and *The Theology of the Book of Revelation* (1993). Elisabeth Schüssler Fiorenza offers liberationist and feminist analyses in her collected essays, *The Book of Revelation: Justice and Judgment* (1985) and in *Revelation: Vision of a Just World* (1991). Walter Wink comments on many passages of Revelation in his *Engaging the Powers* (1992). Christopher Rowland and Mark Corner have written *Liberating Exegesis: The Challenge of Liberation Theology to Biblical Studies* (1989) in which they devote a chapter to the book of Revelation.

In summary I should say that it is hard to know how writers might classify themselves. They might well object to the categories I have proposed. It is certainly far easier to say whether writers are British or American, Catholic or Anglican or Baptist or Lutheran than it is to make them fit neatly into my categories, and a further disclaimer may be in order. These lists are by no means exhaustive.

Issues of Church and World

It is becoming common these days to question the traditional notion that Revelation was originally written in a context of Roman state persecution. John certainly perceived Roman culture as oppressive. In fact he regarded it as posing a mortal danger to Christian faith.

John wrestled with the issue of the relationship between Christian believers and Roman culture. Nothing angered him more than the sight of Christians engaging in business and commerce without a second thought. They joined their non-Christian neighbors in civic celebrations and in the guilds of craftsmen. I imagine they attended the theater, listened to music in the odeon, and cheered their favorites at the games. And perhaps they served on the city council, as Erastus did at Corinth (Rom 16:23). John was fierce in his denunciation not only of the Roman system but also of any fellow Christians who recognized the authority of Roman institutions and supported them actively or passively.

The question of the appropriate Christian relationship to the dominant culture has been answered and is being answered in many different ways. H. R. Niebuhr in *Christ and Culture* (1951) offered a now famous typology of relations between Christ and culture held by Christians over the generations: Christ against Culture, the Christ of Culture, Christ Above Culture, Christ and Culture in Paradox, Christ and the Transformation of Culture.

Douglas Ottati in *Reforming Protestantism: Christian Commitment in Today's World* (1995) argues for a different typology in our generation. He has a vision of churches which are "(1) with the world, confessing our common faults, (2) against the world, criticizing idols and corrupting constrictions, (3) attentive to the world when it exposes their own failures and corruptions, (4) for the world, pursuing a critically constructive and reforming mission to increase the love of God and the neighbor, embody genuine communion, and so equip people to participate faithfully in God's commonwealth" (p. 19). He speaks of a "dynamic relationship" between church and world, as he thinks of the church in, with, against, and for the world, all at the same time. He writes that three other visions of the churches are current rivals of his own notion of the churches as "reforming." Those others he calls churches as "havens for growth groups, as spiritual legitimators of the American way, and as colonies of resident aliens."

Klaus Wengst, *Pax Romana and the Peace of Jesus Christ* (1987), explores various early Christian attitudes toward issues of church and culture, as does Walter Pilgrim, *Uneasy Neighbors: Church and State in the New Testament* (1999). Pilgrim sees three views within the New Testament itself: an ethic of subordination of the church to political structures (Paul, 1 Peter, and Hebrews), an ethic of critical distancing (Jesus and the gospels), and an ethic of resistance (the book of Revelation). It seems to me that the Seer of the book of Revelation positively scorned those fellow Christians of his day who held "an ethic of subordination" or even "an ethic of critical distancing."

Introduction

The Prophet of Patmos and the Artist of Nuremberg

John and His Visions

Late in the first century the prophet John was caught up by the Spirit on the island of Patmos off the western coast of what we today call Turkey. He saw a series of strange visions portending the imminent collapse of the cosmos, the sweeping away of all evil, the final judgment of humankind, and then the glorious descent of the New Jerusalem out of a new heaven to serve as the capital city of a new earth. He committed his visions to writing in the document we call "the book of Revelation" or "the Apocalypse of John."

John's striking visions have fired the imaginations of countless millions in the past and continue to inspire, to puzzle or sometimes to disgust readers up to our own generation.

Revelation is easily the most widely read and the most seriously abused book of the Bible. Precisely because it deals in visions and is chock full of mysterious numbers, symbolic names, monstrous events, beasts and dragons, it has generated controversial and conflicting interpretations.

As I have attempted to unpack the mysteries of the book of Revelation in recent years, I have found help in works of visual art, especially in the art of Albrecht Dürer (1471–1528).

Dürer and His Woodcuts

Almost exactly five hundred years ago, when the printing press was in its infancy, Dürer published at Nuremberg in Germany a bilingual (Latin and German) edition of the Apocalypse and illustrated it with fifteen woodcuts. The images in Dürer's woodcuts capture almost everything in John's Revelation. And they are so compelling in their artistic and spiritual power that they set their stamp on all subsequent generations of illustrators of Revelation.

Dürer was a brilliant draftsman. In his day woodcuts were drawn like cartoons for stained glass windows. They were designed to be filled in with color after being printed in heavy black lines on white paper. But not Dürer's. Instead of merely drawing outlines with plenty of room for color, he revolutionized the process. He made exquisite use of hatching and fine cross lines to evoke a sense of light and shadow. His figures possess a three dimensional quality not seen in his predecessors and rarely achieved by any in his train.

Dürer's drawings refuse to lie still and silent on the page. The book of Revelation is, of course, full of earthquakes and convulsions, terrible voices like peals of thunder or the sound of many waters or the blaring of trumpets, incessant chanting and ecstatic singing, uncontrolled weeping and triumphant cries. The four living creatures surrounding God's throne in Revelation 4 and 5 are not silent sentinels. They bellow, roar, shriek and shout aloud as they lead the cosmic chant, "Holy, Holy, Holy." Dürer is sensitive to all that tumult and passion, and he finds ways to bring it to expression in his work. The energy in his woodcuts is astonishing.

Dürer and John are a good match at many levels. John's language is visionary and highly pictorial. And Dürer with his woodcuts is able to capture the majesty and grotesquery of Revelation in a way that a commentary composed of words alone cannot.

The Artist and the Seer

In his fifteen woodcuts Dürer comments on the central visions of the twenty-one chapters of the book of Revelation. His woodcuts are a splendid pathway into the mysterious Apocalypse. Both in the classroom and in more public gatherings, I have found audiences of all kinds to be remarkably responsive to the intrigue and instruction of these woodcuts. They are an extraordinary aid to grasping the central visions and to being grasped by them. Dürer's work casts a spell over people and draws them into the world of the Apocalypse. The pages that follow are a running commentary both on Dürer's woodcuts and on the whole book of Revelation. I have tried to read the Artist and the Seer simultaneously, letting each throw light on the other.

John experienced his visions in some kind of altered state, woke to write them down, and immediately sent them on their way, desiring to provoke a good response. Dürer's woodcuts are one response. And they are a most admirable response at that. However, at times I believe the Artist fails the Seer, and then I try to point out the tension between them.

Revelation Today

What does Revelation say, and what does it mean? What exactly does it threaten, and does it hold out any promise? Can such a book with its images of a violent God and a wrathful Lamb really be Christian? Is there a correct way to read this book, which speaks so differently to so many people today?

As I weigh the various interpretations of the book of Revelation vying for attention today, I often find myself asking the question of use: "How is John's Revelation being used?" To put it in other terms, "What program or position is an interpreter trying to legitimate or sanction by an appeal to Revelation?"

Three of the uses to which Revelation is put in American Christianity today can be summarized under the labels "fundamentalist," "mainline," and "liberationist."

Fundamentalist Readings

Revelation is required reading, sometimes it seems to be the only reading, among vast numbers of fundamentalist Christians, not only in the United States but around the world.

At one level fundamentalist interpretation seems to be all about date-setting. Preachers and scholars in fundamentalist circles stand in the tradition of John Nelson Darby and the Scofield Bible. They ransack Revelation and the daily newspaper in search of clues for the precise time of such end-time events as the Rapture, the rise of the Antichrist, the Great Tribulation, the Battle of Armageddon, the Second Coming, the Millennium, and the Great White Throne Judgment.

Excitement among these date-setters blazes up whenever some great event appears to fulfil an ancient prophecy. The dawn of the atomic age with the burst of the first atomic bomb in the New Mexico desert in 1945 is greeted as suddenly making possible the kind of mass destruction they see envisioned in Revelation. The establishment of the state of Israel in 1948 means that Jews are returning, as prophesied, to their ancient homeland. The reunification of the city of Jerusalem after the Six Day War in 1967 means that our generation may live to see the rebuilding of the Temple in Jerusalem, foreseen by Ezekiel and presupposed in Jesus' saying about the "desolating sacrilege" in Mark 13:14. The continuing power of Russia, the creation of the European Union (viewed as a revival of the ancient Roman Empire), the rebuilding of Babylon by Saddam Hussein, and continuing unrest in the Middle East are events hailed as foretold in Revelation, as the world plunges towards Armageddon.

Such fundamentalist readings are open to serious criticisms, but here I want to draw special attention to the way these readings are often used. On the one hand, these readings are used to buttress traditional appeals for repentance, calling hearers to distance themselves from the pollutions of a decadent society and summoning them to commit themselves anew to fundamentalist doctrines and to conservative morality.

But more and more in the past quarter century fundamentalist correlations of ancient prophecy and current events have served another use as well, one that is not only personal or churchly but public and political. Interpretation of Revelation has been pressed into the service of right-wing politics.

Back in the days of the Cold War, fundamentalists viewed the peace movement with its call for arms control or disarmament not just as military and political folly but as religious heresies. Peace will never be achieved by human beings, they said. It is a unilateral gift of God to be granted only beyond the battle of Armageddon in the millennium. Until then we are urged to arm ourselves to the teeth.

Even today fundamentalists find that the Russians neatly fill the old biblical role of invaders from the north, while they worry that the huge manpower of China will provide the army of two hundred million invaders crossing the Euphrates from the east (Rev 9:13-17).

Because of Israel's prominence in their understanding of biblical prophecy, including Revelation, fundamentalists lobby the American congress in favor of automatic support for the modern state of Israel. They do so, totally disregarding twenty centuries of history and without any thought for the reality of Arab Christian communities in the Holy Land or for the claims of Muslim Arab communities.

Revelation feeds fundamentalist suspicion of all international religious and political organizations. They see the United Nations and the European Union as part of Satan's design to construct a world government which the Antichrist will ultimately control and use in a final rebellion against God. So those transnational organizations must be opposed. For them the Antichrist is not just a symbol of ever-present evil but is one of our contemporaries, a real human being who perhaps already sits as a member of the European Parliament.

They regard the modern ecumenical movement not as progress but as apostasy, and they fervently believe that such bodies as the World Council of Churches and the worldwide Roman Catholic Church are evolving into the second Beast of the book of Revelation, the false prophet which will make propaganda on behalf of the first Beast, the Antichrist (Rev 13).

Since the demise of the old Soviet Union and the end of the Cold War, some fundamentalists have shifted their energies from a focus on international powers to the power of the American federal government. They see the book of Revelation calling us to arm ourselves (mentally on the part of most or literally on the part of militias) against a monstrous Big Government slouching across the horizon out of Wall Street and Washington, intent on destroying the sovereignty of the American nation and curbing the freedom of individual citizens.

Some believe that the Federal Government has plans to perform surgery and implant into our hands or head the mark of the beast (Rev 13:16) in the form of tiny computer chips. That will enable the government to track our every movement and monitor our every purchase (Rev 13:16-17). They fear that the Federal Government wants to control our thinking and will take drastic steps to prevent us from practicing our Christian faith and will try to compel us to worship the Antichrist. So they read Revelation as a call to aggressive resistance.

The Mainline and Revelation

More conservative elements among the mainline churches read the book of Revelation as visions to be interpreted in keeping with the traditional Christian scheme of things as set out, for example, in the ancient creeds. Those creeds speak of Jesus as having ascended into heaven, where he is now seated at the right hand of God. At the end of human history he will come to judge the living and dead. When he comes in glory, all the dead will be resurrected, and the saints will begin to enjoy the life of the world to come. The creeds provide a template for reading Revelation.

More liberal elements among the mainstream have trouble with the traditional pictures of a literal second coming of Christ and all that it entails. For a long time they have sought refuge in symbolic readings of those ancient images.

Mainline denominations in the tradition of Luther and Calvin, who held a low opinion of the book of Revelation, seem inclined to leave this book to one side, finding it more confusing than useful. When absolutely pressed to deal with Revelation, preachers in these churches often focus their energies on the letters to the Seven Churches (Rev 2–3), finding in them some grist for their homiletical mills. But they have tended to ignore the dark and enigmatic visions of the following chapters (Rev 6–20) as not being particularly useful for constructive ethical and spiritual ends.

Artists and musicians are always an exception and so also here. They have long found inspiration in the angelic songs and anthems of Revelation (such as 5:9-14), and snatches of the hymnody of Revelation began to turn up in the liturgies of the mainstream a long time ago. The most intuitive and poetic souls in mainstream churches have always found themselves attracted to Revelation for some of the same reasons that the Reformers were repelled. They testify that the strange and powerful images of Revelation, so repulsive to many, work in their own minds to revitalize their imaginations and their language, shattering easy assumptions, unveiling realities that transcend the commonplace, causing scales to fall from their eyes so that they behold the majesty of God once more.

Recently many in the mainstream have begun to take a second and a third look at Revelation as a whole, sometimes for no better reason than the fact that they fear abandoning their constituencies to what they regard as the bizarre and even dangerous interpretations of the fundamentalists.

On the basis of extensive historical study of ancient apocalyptic materials over the past century, the nightmarish images of Revelation that offended or confused readers in Reformation times (such as blood running from the winepress of God's wrath in a river as deep as a horse's bridle, Rev 14:17-20) are now seen to be stock images of apocalyptic. They are certainly not to be read literally.

The mainstream has always insisted that Revelation is an example of biblical prophecy. That does not mean that it is a prediction of events to occur in some distant future, long centuries after the prophet's death.

Revelation is not a page out of God's appointment book, telling us in advance when the end will come and what events will immediately precede it. Revelation is prophetic testimony aimed at John's contemporaries, and we must read Revelation by peering over the prophet's shoulder to see what he was saying to his own generation. Then we can begin to draw out some implications for our own situation.

Others in the mainline insist that Revelation must be read not only in its historical context but also in its literary context as the last book of the Bible. Revelation is the powerful and appropriate conclusion to the great drama that begins in Genesis. The whole notion of the human being as "the time being," as an actor located on a timeline between creation and new creation, living from God as source and heading towards God as our end and goal, owes everything to the inclusion of the book of Revelation as the final book in the library of books called Holy Scripture.

Revelation plays a vital role in the lives of readers inhabiting a confused and confusing world where personal and political tragedies are vividly reported on the evening news or spill over into our direct experience. Revelation strips the mask from the notion that ours is a one dimensional universe and that we are one dimensional beings adrift in a mechanical cosmos. Revelation shows us the Lamb of God, the throne of God, and the coming triumph of God. Ours is a fallen and dangerous world. But Revelation teaches us that we are living, not towards death but towards God, towards the new creation, towards the New Jerusalem (Rev 21–22).

Liberationist Readings of Revelation

An increasingly influential reading of Revelation is provided by liberationist interpreters. The word "revelation" itself provides an entrée to their views.

Everyone agrees that "Revelation" or "Apocalypse" means unveiling. But what exactly is unveiled or revealed? Fundamentalists see Revelation as unveiling the precise details of God's timetable for the last days of planet earth. Mainline interpreters see Revelation as pulling aside for a moment the dark veil hiding God's bright sovereignty from our eyes.

Liberationists understand "Revelation" not simply as an "unveiling" of hidden truths about God's present and future rule. They think of "Revelation" as an "unmasking" of the dominant mode of the structuring of power in our world. In New Testament times the system which dominated the cities and countries where Christians lived was the Roman Empire. This empire not only controlled the material resources but also de-

manded nothing less than total allegiance from its inhabitants. Revelation exposes Rome as a cultural, economic, and political system favoring the rich, the powerful, and the well-connected. Revelation unmasks the empire and exposes it as the enemy rather than the benefactor of the vast majority of its citizens. At the same time Revelation unmasks the majority of Christians as all too happy to cooperate with the state instead of resisting the dominant ideology.

Far and away the most common reading of Revelation 12–13, inside and outside of liberationist circles, is that the Seer is denouncing the Roman imperial system by calling it the Beast summoned up from the sea by the Dragon. The Dragon is explicitly declared to be the ancient serpent also known as the Devil or Satan (Rev 12:9). Where liberationists differ from the mainstream is in their insistence that any interpretation of Revelation is fatally flawed if it does not understand that the apocalyptic Beast has its counterpart and continuation today in the international political and financial system of the industrialized world. The current dominant system is the Beast in the way it deals with Third World peoples, and in the way the First World rides roughshod over the poor for the sake of putting obscene profits into the pockets of CEOs and a few favored investors.

John saw a second Beast rising up from the land, and it enticed people to worship the first Beast (Rev 13:11). In our own day, say liberationists, this second Beast is the dominant ideology or myth seducing us to believe that the present economic system deserves our support because it is time-honored, or because it is sanctioned by the Bible, or because it benefits everyone who is honest and willing to work. This myth whispers to us that unemployment, poverty, and the degrading of God's green earth are small side effects of a system which yields blessings in greater abundance than any problems it dumps in its wake. In fact the system dispenses a stream of consumer goods to the relatively well-off, lulling them into spiritual slumber.

Liberationists sharply criticize the leaders of mainline churches. Mainline churches, they say, are filled with sleepy members of the prosperous middle class. If they do not wake up, they deserve the name of Beast. Mainline Christian leaders should be unmasking the satanic reality of the dominant system and working to undo its oppressions. Instead they devote their energies to bringing meaning into the lives of their comfortable but confused memberships, while they neglect the real social, economic, and political ills of our nation and planet.

Revelation echoes and re-echoes with voices crying out for justice and vengeance. Many in mainline churches are troubled by the language of vengeance in the book of Revelation and deplore it. Liberationists, however, defend the saints' prayers for vengeance (Rev 6:10) and their celebrations of the wrathful responses of God and Lamb (Rev 19:1-4) as the natural and indeed legitimate outcries of oppressed and marginalized people being ground up by the prevailing domination system.

So liberationists criticize fundamentalists for recommending that we all wait patiently for God's future kingdom in heaven instead of incarnating and articulating God's sovereignty now on the earth. When fundamentalists enter the public sphere, as they are doing increasingly, liberationists accuse them of idolizing the free market system and America's role in international politics.

Liberationists criticize mainline churches for offering bandaids and sympathy to the victims of the dominant system instead of standing with them in solidarity and co-suffering.

Feminist Interpretation

Among liberationist readers, feminist interpreters have in particular leveled sharp criticism against two aspects of the imagery of the Apocalypse. In the first place, they object that Revelation offers caricatures of women rather than realistic portraits. They point to the way John puts the Heavenly Woman (Rev 12) on a pedestal, and then on the other hand demonizes the prophetess called "Jezebel" (Rev 2) and uses the image of the Great Harlot as a symbol of the evil empire in Revelation 17.

In addition, feminist interpreters have been in the front ranks of those who alert us to dangers in the way Revelation describes the kingdom of God as a hierarchical system in which God and the Lamb overcome their enemies through sheer power, making war on their opponents and destroying them, rather than reconciling their enemies through forgiveness and compassion.

Many besides feminists find the language of Revelation distressing. What image of God, of Christ, and of the reign of God do we find in Revelation? And does it measure up to the highest and best that we have in New Testament portraits of God and Christ?

The Apocalyptic Visions of Revelation

The book of Revelation brims with eerie nightmarish images: locusts like horses arrayed for battle with human faces and scorpions' tails (9:1-11); blood running from the winepress of God's wrath in a terrible river as deep as a horse's bridle (14:17-20); the sea and the rivers and all the springs of the earth turned to fountains of blood (16:3-7); three foul spirits like frogs issuing from the mouths of the dragon and the beast and the false prophet (16:13); all the birds of the air gathered to eat the flesh of fallen kings in a grim feast (19:17-18).

It is easy to sympathize with those who claim that this book knows only the shadow side of God and draws a curtain across God's infinite compassion. Deadly images of destruction are portrayed at such length and with such vivid detail that they threaten to overwhelm our imaginations.

Here at the close of our century and millennium, the word "apocalyptic" is commonplace, even among people who never go to church and have never read the book of Revelation. For at least the last fifty years secular prophets have warned us of coming global disaster resulting from nuclear war, chemicals in our food supply, destruction of the rain forests, global warming, depletion of the ozone layer, and the onslaught of new and deadlier viruses. Those gloomy forecasts have been dubbed "secular apocalypses."

So today the word "apocalyptic" has come to signify some combination of "catastrophic" and "deeply pessimistic." The book of Revelation and Dürer's woodcuts, however, are brimming with hope. Both the Seer and the Artist express their deep conviction that the struggles of the faithful are leading not to Doomsday and meltdown, but to the kingdom of God.

Both John the Seer and Dürer the Artist strive to center our imaginations not on darkness but on God. The dominant image in Revelation is the throne of God and so the sovereignty of God. It is vain for earthly governors or governments to oppose God, and it is folly for people to fear those earthly governments rather than God. God has placed the present and the future into the hands of the Lamb. The course of human history remains a mystery, and is shrouded at times in deep darkness. But Revelation is clear that the last word of God and the Lamb is not darkness but light, not death but life. The final vision in the book of Revelation is not of a burned out cinder of a planet. It is rather the vision of a New Heaven and a New Earth.

Great value is assigned also to the deeds of human beings. The faith and hope, the testimony and deeds, the resistance and suffering of the faithful are not in vain. They are seen by the all-seeing God, valued by God, and taken up into the purpose of God, who will give the New Creation. "Blessed are the dead who die in the Lord, . . . for they go forth with their deeds!" (Rev 14:13).

Chapter 1

A Synopsis of the Book of Revelation

No simple outline can possibly capture the kaleidoscope of images and visions in the book of Revelation. Nevertheless a synopsis, not to be confused with the Apocalypse itself, might help orient us in our reading.

1:1-8 John introduces himself and his book. God gave him "the revelation of Jesus Christ" through an angel, and he pronounces a blessing on all who heed the message.

1:9–3:22 On the island of Patmos one Lord's Day John was "in the Spirit" and was granted a vision of Jesus, not as Jesus existed in his earthly ministry, but as the exalted One, who was dead but now lives forever and has power over Death and Hades. In a voice like a trumpet Christ dictates to John seven letters for the Seven Churches of Asia Minor (1:9-20).

The seven messages contain praise and blame, threat and promise, and they reveal the basic values of the Christ of the Apocalypse. Various churches are blamed for abandoning their first love, for complacency, for tolerating false apostles, for lukewarmness. They are praised insofar as they exhibit any sign of fidelity, patient endurance, or intolerance toward evildoers and false teachers like Jezebel and the Nicolaitans. The faithful in the churches are promised a share in the glorious life to come in the New Jerusalem (2:1–3:22).

4:1–22:5 John reports further visions. Many of John's visions are organized in sets of seven. The sets do not follow one another in neat chronological order. Instead, each series of seven visions parallels the others. However, each succeeding series does not simply repeat what the preceding series showed. We find growing intensity and increasing emphasis on the final members of the series as we read through the book.

And at various moments an individual series is interrupted by a visionary interlude.

4:1–7:17 Seven seals. The Seer is caught up into heaven where he sees "One seated on the throne," surrounded by four living creatures and twenty-four elders (4:1-11). He watches as the Lamb, slaughtered and yet living again, takes from God's hand a mysterious scroll sealed with seven seals. Suddenly the whole cosmos breaks out in doxologies, praising God and the Lamb (5:1-14).

The Lamb begins to break the seals, setting in motion colossal events on earth and in heaven: the Four Horsemen begin their terrible ride (6:1-8), apparently as punishment upon those who killed the martyred souls now crying out beneath heaven's altar (6:9-11), the earth quakes and the sun is darkened (6:12-17). Then, following visions of the 144,000 servants of God sealed on their foreheads and of a countless multitude out of every nation (7:1-17), the snapping of the seventh seal brings not the end we expect but a further set of visions (8:1).

8:1–11:19 Seven angels blow seven trumpets, setting in motion six disasters greater than those accompanying the snapping of the seals (8:2–9:21). After the sixth trumpet John sees a great angel with a little open scroll (10:1-11), the measuring of the temple (11:1-2), and the drama of the two witnesses (11:3-14). When the seventh trumpet blares, we seem to be carried forward to the end of the world as loud voices in heaven praise God for judging the nations and rewarding the saints (11:15-19). But the book does not end yet.

12:1–13:18 The Dragon and the Beasts. A Heavenly Woman, clothed with the sun, is about to give birth. She is menaced by the Great Red Dragon but

1

escapes with heaven's help (12:1-6). Then John sees War in Heaven with Michael and his angels casting the Dragon out of heaven and down onto the earth (12:7-12), whereupon the Dragon goes off to make war on the Woman's children, the Christian community (12:13-17).

The Dragon (the Devil) summons two beasts, one from the sea, one from the land, to act as his agents in his warfare on God's people. The first beast is usually identified as "the Antichrist" (although the name "Antichrist" never actually appears in Revelation). The second beast makes people worship the first beast and bear its mark. And the number of the first beast is 666 (13:1-18).

14:1-20   Seven angels of judgment. First we are shown 144,000 redeemed, victorious in heaven, singing a new song and following the Lamb wherever he goes (14:1-5). These all resisted the beast. Then John sees a series of Seven Angels announcing judgment, beginning with God's judgment on Babylon and those who have the mark of the beast. The series continues until the wine of God's wrath flows like a terrible river (14:6-20).

15:1–16:21   Seven bowls of wrath. Seven angels emerge from the heavenly temple bearing bowls "brimming with the wrath of God" (15:1-8). The bowls are poured out like the plagues in the days of Pharaoh and Moses. As the sixth bowl is outpoured, the kings and nations of the earth gather against God at Armageddon (16:16), thinking it is their day, but the day belongs to God the Almighty. The pouring out of the seventh bowl announces judgment on Babylon (16:17-21), and that judgment is detailed in the following two chapters.

17:1–19:10   Babylon. One of the seven angels shows John a woman with the mysterious name "Babylon." She is called "the Mother of all Whores" (17:5). We are told that the woman is a city set on seven hills (17:9), and that must mean that this city is Rome, even though the name "Rome" never appears in Revelation. The woman-city, enemy of God's people, boasts that she is an eternal city, but in spite of her power and wealth she is overthrown "in an hour" (18:9, 17). At the fall of Babylon, heaven breaks out in a wild chorus of mighty Alleluias (19:1-10).

19:11–22:5   New Jerusalem. Christ ("The Word of God" who is "King of kings and Lord over all lords") descends at the head of heaven's armies (19:11-16). The beast and the false prophet are thrown into the lake of fire (19:17-21). The dragon is cast into the bottomless pit for a thousand years (20:1-3). Martyrs are resurrected to reign with Christ (20:4-6). At the end of the thousand years the dragon is released and leads one last doomed rebellion. He is immediately defeated and cast into the lake of fire (20:7-10). Then all the dead are raised and appear before the judgment seat of God (20:11-15). Finally John sees a new heaven and a new earth, and he tours the New Jerusalem which descends from heaven as an eternal habitation for the people of God (21:1–22:5).

22:6-21   Revelation closes as it opened, with words intended to impress on readers the authority of the Seer and the urgency of heeding his summons to an undivided loyalty to God and Christ. Once more, as in the beginning, John promises blessing on everyone who keeps the words of his prophetic book and again declares that Jesus is coming soon (1:3; 22:7).

John's Revelation and Dürer's Woodcuts

The book of Revelation has twenty-two chapters, and Dürer produced fifteen woodcuts, plus an introductory cameo. The chart below shows how the chapters and the woodcuts are related and where to find them in this book.

REVELATION	*WOODCUTS*
Rev 1:1-3	Cameo: John, Prophet and Seer
Rev 1:9	1 The Persecution of the Seer
Rev 1:9–3:22	2 John's First Vision and The Seven Letters
Rev 4:1–5:14	3 Heaven's Throne Room
Rev 6:1-8	4 The Four Horsemen
Rev 6:9-17	5 Opening the Fifth and Sixth Seals
Rev 7:1-17	6 The Seal of the Living God
Rev 8:1-13	7 Seven Angels with Seven Trumpets
Rev 9:1-21	8 The Fifth and Sixth Trumpets
Rev 10–11	9 Another Mighty Angel
Rev 12:1-6, 13-17	10 The Woman and the Dragon
Rev 12:7-12	11 War in Heaven
Rev 13:1-18	12 The Beast Whose Number is 666
Rev 14:1-5	13 The New Song of the 144,000
Rev 14:6–16:21	[Seven Angels of Judgment and Seven Angels with Seven Plagues]*
Rev 17:1–19:10	14 Babylon, Mother of All Whores
Rev 19:11–22:21	15 Binding of Satan and the New Jerusalem

*Dürer did not dedicate a separate woodcut to the Seven Angels of Judgment and the Seven Angels with the Seven Plagues.

Chapter 2

Revelation 1:1-3
John, Prophet and Seer

For the 1511 edition of his illustrated *Apocalypse,* Dürer produced one new woodcut, a cameo representing John offering his finished book of prophecy to the Virgin and Child.

John, Prophet and Seer
(Rev 1:1-3)

Dürer prefaced the 1511 edition of his work on the book of Revelation with a small woodcut. In it he pictures John gazing up at the Virgin Mary holding the Christ child. The eagle at John's elbow is the Seer's well-known symbol, traditional since the days of the early church. That eagle is one of the "four living creatures" around the throne of God (see Rev 4:6).

Unfortunately, Dürer's eagle seems scrawny and looks too much like a plucked chicken to inspire awe. The eagle is cackling or shrieking a cry of celebration. John's work is over. He has finished writing his book. He still holds his pen, but he has set aside his inkwell and laid it on the rock.

John leans to his left and directs his gaze upward to the Virgin Mary enthroned in heavenly glory above the slender crescent of the moon. She wears a crown of stars and seems to be none other than the heavenly woman of Revelation 12. Light streams from her. Or is it from the Child she holds? Perhaps the two are simply inseparable in Dürer's mind. The infant has one hand on Mary's shoulder, and with the other he chucks her chin in an act of tender love. John lifts his hand, dedicating his book to the Virgin and her Child.

By picturing John and Mary with her Child all floating on clouds, Dürer lifts them up out of ordinary space and offers them to us as objects of adoration and spiritual meditation. That is exactly how John wanted to be treated.

In the opening paragraph of Revelation (1:1-3) John lays claim to a unique authority. His book, he says, is not a mere personal word based on a subjective analysis of the situation. Nor is it the product of study in some library or discussion with colleagues. He is a prophet and no ordinary author. He did not labor to produce his book. It was all given to him, he says, as a "revelation." "Revelation" is a Latin word. The underlying Greek word has come into English as "Apocalypse." Both words mean an unveiling. And John says that he is the one chosen by God to see what lies on the other side of the veil and to communicate it to the Seven Churches.

Who is it that makes this claim to be a Seer? Old tradition has it that one and the same John composed the Fourth Gospel, the three Epistles bearing John's name, and the book of Revelation. This John, says the tradition, was the brother of James, the son of Zebedee, none other than the Beloved Disciple. Some ancients like Dionysius of Alexandria and many modern students of the Johannine writings deny that a single author composed all five of these documents because of perceived differences in language, tone, and outlook. There's no need for us to take sides in this dispute. The author of Revelation identifies himself simply as "John" (1:1, 4, 8; 22:8), and he speaks of his work as a book of "prophecy" (1:3; 22:7, 10, 18, 19). Therefore I will simply call him John, along with referring to him as "the Seer" or "the Prophet."

John surrounds his words with the aura of divine authority, just as Dürer lifts John up into the clouds. However, many ancient and modern readers have plucked John and his book out of the clouds and set them down squarely on the earth. In spite of John's high claims, the book of Revelation made its way into the Christian Bible only slowly. Its inclusion as one of the Christian holy books was opposed for a variety of reasons. Many like Dionysius denied that it had been penned by an apostle. Others were repulsed by its physical description of the life of the world to come, preferring more spiritual images. In the Reformation period Martin Luther found it lacking in good news and in clarity, and he regarded the Seer's claims as egotistical. Luther objected that the Seer goes "much too far when he commends his own book so highly" in passages like Rev 1:3 and 22:18-19.

It seems important to ponder the function of the Seer's opening paragraph. The Seer claims divine authority for his work, because he is involved in a controversy with other Christian teachers and prophets about the proper way of relating to the secular culture of their day. What the Seer is basically saying is that his own opinion is correct (indeed divine) and that other

Christian responses to the situation are incorrect and even demon-inspired. It is very hard to argue with a person who makes assertions on the basis of visions and the voices of angels.

The Seer did not want anyone to talk back or disagree with him. He desired obedience. He expected his book to be read spiritually, in the midst of the gathered community, as a word from God, and he pronounces a benediction upon lector and hearers (Rev 1:3). Getting a blessing out of the book of Revelation has never been easy, but that is what the following pages attempt to lay hold of. And I will venture sometimes to say "yes" and sometimes "no" to various assertions of the book of Revelation.

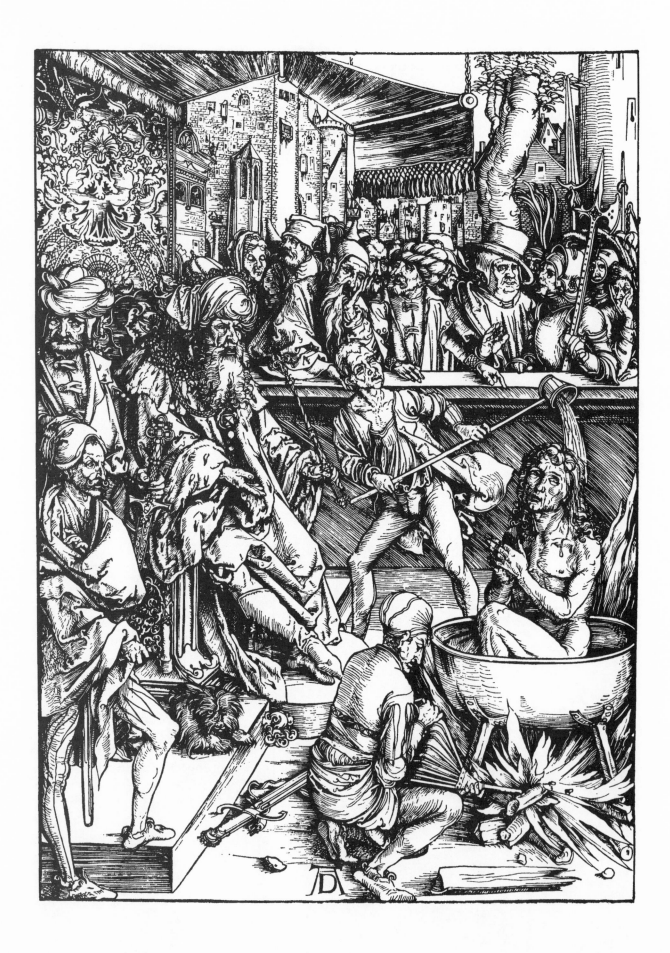

Chapter 3

Revelation 1:9

The Persecution of the Seer

Dürer here illustrates an apocryphal scene: John in a pot of boiling oil in front of the Roman emperor. Tradition has it that John was arrested in Ephesus and taken to Rome for trial. Unable to kill John, who enjoyed divine protection, the emperor exiled him to the island of Patmos. Even though this scene is not part of the book of Revelation, it is a most appropriate introduction to a book whose pages are packed with visionary descriptions of God's Holy War against evil. In the book of Revelation, that spiritual warfare breaks out in the world of space and time as a sharp conflict between Christ and culture, between church and empire.

The Persecution of the Seer
(Rev 1:9)

The event pictured here is no part of the text of Revelation but something like this is widely assumed to lie behind the writing of the Apocalypse. According to an old Christian story, John refused to sacrifice to the emperor's image in Ephesus. He was therefore arrested and taken to Rome to be tried at the imperial court. After hearing the charges, Domitian (emperor from A.D. 81–96) condemned John to be boiled in oil. An early sixteenth-century church, bearing the graphic name of San Giovanni in Olio ("St. John in Oil"), marks the spot in Rome to this day!

Dürer unfolds the scene. Seated beneath a brocade baldachino, the emperor Domitian slouches forward, holding in one hand his ceremonial scepter and with the other offering a weary gesture of command, ordering the execution of the Seer. Dürer places a turban on Domitian's head, making him look just like Dürer's contemporary, the Turkish sultan. Of course it would never do to assign the role of persecutor of the church to Maximilian I, the late fifteenth century "Holy Roman Emperor," even if he was the legal successor of Domitian. After all, Maximilian was Dürer's patron, and anyway the Turks were the prime threat to Christian Europe in Dürer's day. In 1453, a mere forty-five years before Dürer produced his Apocalypse (1498), Constantinople, the capital of the Byzantine Christian empire, had fallen to the Turks, and by Dürer's own day Turkish armies had pressed forward to the gates of Vienna.

Nevertheless, except for the emperor-sultan and his counselor, all the people crowding around to view the execution are a wonderful cross section neither of ancient Rome nor of the Turkish Empire. They are all "good citizens" of Dürer's own German society. Their faces and hands, their hats and robes, coats and cloaks, armor and helmets, are individually drawn with loving attention to the detail of late fifteenth-century life in northern Europe. Here Dürer is not just drawing. He is preaching. In his opinion, not only the Turkish sultan but also these solid German citizens are guilty of ignoring or suppressing the truth and of retarding the advent of the new age. They stand idly by, giving tacit approval to the ruler's act of persecution. They excuse their passive inaction by saying, "It's none of our business," or "The emperor knows best," or "We don't want any trouble." That is precisely the attitude Revelation condemns. Both the Artist and the Seer summon readers to discern the demons behind the oppressive acts of governments and to resist them with all their might.

The emperor-sultan and most of these same people make a second appearance in woodcut number 14 (see also 12), where they stand exposed as worshipers of the whore of Babylon.

All the faces in the woodcut are wonderfully drawn. Behind Domitian stands his turbaned counselor. He has urged this execution but doubt is written all over his face. The counselor doubts, the emperor displays utter contempt, and the captain of the guard, gripping the hasp of his sword, directs the execution. A soldier has laid his weapon to one side and is all business. He squats before the fire and stokes it up with a bellows. A slave-boy feels the heat on his face and leans back as he pours oil over the kneeling Seer.

John kneels in the tub of oil and prays. He is set off-center on the right side of the composition, and he looks away to his left. If our eyes follow the direction of his gaze, we are led to the next woodcut, which depicts the opening vision of the Apocalypse. By this device, Dürer says that the martyr fixes his eyes not on the earthly emperor, seated on his throne beneath all that brocade, but on the exalted Christ seated on the clouds of heaven. And so should all of us.

Domitian's turbaned counselor is also staring off toward the next picture, and he has a worried look on his face. I think he has begun to question whether he gave correct advice to the emperor. Of the eighteen pairs of eyes in the picture only those of the dog at Domitian's feet stare directly at us. That scowling terrier senses the presence of God, the way animals are said to sense a coming earthquake.

Revelation *1:9*

According to the legend, the boiling oil could not hurt John. In another version of the old legend, John was condemned to drink poison. But either way, neither poison nor boiling oil had any ill effect on him whatsoever. In astonishment and disgust the emperor banished John to the island of Patmos, off the coast of Asia Minor (Western Turkey today), about forty miles southwest of Ephesus.

Although the attempt to execute John by boiling him in oil is not narrated in the book of Revelation, Dürer's decision to open his series with this particular picture is a masterstroke. It captures the air of menace and antagonism hovering over the book of Revelation. At the beginning of his book, John describes himself as sharing three things with the people to whom he writes, and these three are a significant trio. He says he shares with them (1) persecution, (2) the kingdom, and (3) patience (Rev 1:9).

"Persecution" could mean official actions like arrest, examination under torture, jailing, and execution. However, the underlying Greek word could be translated "pressure," and that would carry a somewhat different sense of the situation. The Roman Empire and Roman society surely exerted pressure on all inhabitants to conform to Roman customs and Roman ideas, including ritual adoration of the emperor as divine and of Roma as a goddess.

In addition to feeling the same pressure, the Seer reminds his audience that he shares with them "the kingdom." That is to say, he and all other Christians trust in God's own "kingship" or imperial "sovereignty." Revelation defines the Christians as a body of citizens over whom God reigns (1:6). The Seer emphasizes that God's sovereignty, unlike Rome's, is everlasting, omnipotent, and holy. He punctuates his narrative with hymns and doxologies sung to God by angels and all creatures, thereby inviting his readers to add their own voices, as pledges of their allegiance (e.g., Rev 4:9-11).

Thirdly, besides "pressure" and "the kingdom," John writes that he shares "patience" with his believing sisters and brothers. "Patience" means enduring hard times in the conviction that God's sovereignty will soon be manifested. "Patience" could be taken to mean passive waiting, a timid ducking of the head, a quiet hanging in there. But "patience" includes active, determined "resistance" to the allure and pressure exerted by the dominant culture.

John then goes on to say that he was "on the island of Patmos because of the word of God and the testimony to Jesus" (1:9).

But Was John a Prisoner of Rome?

The usual interpretation of John's situation is that the Roman authorities had decided to silence John's teaching and preaching by removing him from his home in Ephesus and imprisoning him on Patmos.

A very different interpretation is possible. It could be that John was not banished by the Romans but left Ephesus on his own initiative, sailing off to Patmos and other islands in order to evangelize and organize there just as he had worked in mainland cities. For several reasons I have begun to listen seriously to this latter interpretation.

In the first place, the traditional view that Domitian was a fierce and systematic persecutor of the church has recently been called into question. Furthermore, no ancient evidence exists that Patmos ever served as a prison colony, although it is true that other islands in the Aegean were known to have housed prisoners of the Roman state.

Secondly, when John writes to the Seven Churches and describes their condition (Rev 2–3), he has a little to say about persecution (2:10, 13), but it is very little. The opponents John identifies are predominantly internal. The Seven Churches are being preyed upon, he says, by errant Christian prophets whom he calls false apostles (2:2), Nicolaitans (2:6, 15), Balaamites (2:14) and Jezebel (2:20). As John himself describes his situation, he points to controversy inside the Christian community and not to persecution from outsiders.

Thirdly, we need to read John's own claim carefully. John says that he was on Patmos "because of the word of God and testimony to Jesus" (1:9). These words are usually taken as proof that he was exiled to Patmos. But the words could mean that he left Ephesus, not because of pressure from Roman authorities but of his own free will and by his own design. Clearly John was embroiled in controversy with other Christian leaders. It could very well be that, angered by the indifference or opposition of many Christians in the seven cities, he sailed off to Patmos and other islands in hopes of finding more fertile ground for his teachings.

What is beyond dispute is that John spent time on Patmos. There on that dry and sparsely peopled island, John had his visions. Whatever his circumstances, he enjoyed sufficient freedom to write them down and send them off to the circle of Seven Churches on the mainland. The persecution tradition says that John was freed when Domitian died. The new emperor declared many of Domitian's decrees to be null and void, and political prisoners of the old regime were released. Presumably John returned to Ephesus, where he once more took up his contested leadership among the Seven Churches.

Freed by His Blood *(1:5)*

Whether John had actually experienced persecution up to the time of writing, he certainly expected it for himself and for the churches some time in the near future. In his Revelation he glorifies martyrdom. He represents Jesus himself as a martyr, "the faithful witness" who "freed us by his blood" (1:5). John's favorite title for Jesus is "the Lamb," and he describes the Lamb as standing alive and triumphant but still bearing the marks of slaughter (5:6). And John says that when Christ returns in power, all who "pierced" him will see him (1:7).

Furthermore, John exalts martyrs as the ideal for all Christians. Those beneath the altar crying out, "How long, Lord?" are those who, like Jesus, have been "killed on account of the word of God" (6:9). The innumerable host before the throne, arrayed in white with palm branches in their hands, are those who have "washed their robes in the blood of the Lamb" (7:14). Those who conquered the Devil are those "whose love of life did not cause them to shrink back from death" (12:11). Those who were "because of their witness to Jesus" and did not receive the mark of the beast are the ones who will reign with Christ for a thousand years (20:4-6).

John everywhere lifts up martyred saints as examples. And yet he can name only one martyr among the Seven Churches, namely Antipas of Pergamum (2:13), an obscure and otherwise unknown figure.

Obviously John himself had not yet given his life. Of course, with every word that he writes, he insists that he is ready and willing to do so. It seems to me that John was a stern soldier in ancient culture wars. All his references to slaughter and blood are designed to scold and shame lax or wavering or lukewarm Christians in the Seven Churches. In John's eyes, some in the churches are perceptive and faithful, but far too many fail to understand that they are involved in a spiritual warfare and are being called to active resistance, even to the point of yielding up their lives. To John the churches seem to be too much at home in their seven cities, far too uncritical of Roman culture, much too willing to go along and get along.

Besides scolding, the Seer encourages. If the Christians of the seven cities resist the pressure to conform their lives to the values and currents of Roman culture, they will surely suffer for it. They will feel the wrath of Rome, perhaps in official actions, perhaps in the derision and contempt of their neighbors. No matter. John's Revelation insists that the entire Roman system, indeed the whole of human society and culture as we know it, is doomed (see especially Rev 13–17). But on the other hand, all faithful resisters, even if they are martyred, will secure a place in the New Jerusalem (Rev 21–22). Once more John uses the language of warfare when he says that Jesus as Lion and Lamb has won and will win "victory" (5:5; 17:14). And then he says that all the faithful will in God's good time be revealed as "victors" (Rev 2:7, 11, 17, 26; 3:5, 12, 21; 21:7; cf. 12:11; 15:2). Their names are already written in the book of Life (3:5; 20:15).

Dürer's opening woodcut with John in a cauldron of boiling oil offers a scene nowhere to be found in the book of Revelation. Still it turns out to be a perfect introduction to a book brimming with images of martyrdom and calling Christians to resist the power and blandishments of the dominant culture, even to the giving of their lives.

Chapter 4

Revelation 1:9–3:22

John's First Vision and the Seven Letters

One Lord's Day on the barren island called Patmos, John was granted a vision of the exalted Jesus Christ. What does John see? Not the Jesus of the Gospels, receiving outcasts, eating with tax collectors and sinners, touching lepers, uttering parables of the shepherd seeking one lost sheep or the father running to embrace the prodigal son. Rather John sees a mighty Christ, resurrected from the dead, a sharp sword protruding from his mouth with power over Death and Hades.

This Jesus strides purposefully in the midst of the seven golden lampstands which are the Seven Churches of Asia Minor, and he dictates seven messages to the Seven Churches: Ephesus, Smyrna, Pergamum, Thyatira, Sardis, Philadelphia, and Laodicea.

The seven messages reveal the basic values of the Christ of the Apocalypse and serve as a window opening onto the situation of Christians living at the end of the first century in western Asia Minor. Various churches are criticized for aban-doning their first love, for growing complacent, for tolerating false apostles, for lukewarmness. They are praised insofar as they exhibit any sign of fidelity, patient endurance, or intolerance toward evildoers and false teachers.

It is remarkable that these messages have little to say about any persecution of Christians by the Roman Empire. The Devil is poised to "throw some into prison" (2:10; cf. 3:10), and one Christian is known to have been martyred under circumstances which are never described (2:13). Nevertheless, John represents Christ as addressing not a situation of oppression or persecution for Christians but rather one of their comfort and ease in the midst of a pagan culture. Assimilation or accommodation and not persecution is the primary issue addressed by these seven messages.

Christians are called in these messages and everywhere in Revelation to a strenuous fidelity. Only the faithful will share in the glorious life to come in the New Jerusalem.

Dürer pictures John in the presence of the exalted Christ, almost exactly as John himself reports his experience. Nevertheless the differences between Dürer and John are intriguing.

John's First Vision
and the Seven Letters
(Rev 1:9–3:22)

On the Lord's Day *(1:9)*

One Lord's Day toward the end of the first century John was overwhelmed by a vision of the exalted Jesus. John reports hearing a loud voice like a trumpet, and when he turned toward the voice, he saw a great human-like figure standing in the midst of seven golden lampstands (1:9-12).

One Like the Son of Man *(1:13-20)*

Dürer captures John's description wonderfully well. As the exalted Christ dominates the first chapter of Revelation, so a majestic Christ dominates Dürer's woodcut. In vitality and power Christ far outshines the earthly emperor portrayed in the preceding woodcut. Here the exalted Christ sits erect and confident, staring directly at us, in fact stabbing at us with terrible eyes brooding beneath brows of flame. Trinitarian rays of light stream from his head. His face burns like the pitiless Mediterranean sun at high noon. In fact, Dürer's composition is not simply circular but is clock-like. Christ's head is situated precisely at twelve o'clock. We are put on notice that time is running out on the world's clock. The day of God's judgment is drawing relentlessly nearer, and we should fear God and God's word rather than the edicts of earthly sovereigns.

As he labors to render his ecstatic experience in words, John borrows images from older biblical visions, especially the visions of the Ancient of Days and the Son of Man in Daniel 7 and of the archangel in Daniel 10. Like those figures, John's Christ is a mighty warrior, ready to do battle against the enemies of God's people in a Holy War.

Ancient coins picture Roman emperors wearing a radiate crown, like the Christ of Revelation. Those coins and their inscriptions proclaim the emperors to be the source of divine light for the whole civilized world. The Seer opposes that imperial pretension and declares that Christ is the one supreme source of saving and civilizing light. His head and hair are white as snow, brilliant and blinding as the sun, while his eyes blaze like fires (1:14). He stands on feet of burnished bronze (1:15), not feet of clay (Dan 2:33-34), and he is immovable.

This awesome figure addressing John is clearly the crucified and resurrected Jesus Christ. He identifies himself to John with the words, "I am the first and the last, and the living one. I was dead, but look! I am alive forever and ever" (1:17-18).

Working not with words but with knife and ink on wood, Dürer seems to echo sculptures and windows of great medieval cathedrals with their fearful scenes of the last judgment carved in stone or captured in stained glass. John and Dürer both describe Jesus as mighty Warrior and as Judge of the Universe.

Dürer's Christ is enthroned above a double rainbow. He sits on one bow and rests his slippered feet on another. But from his mouth there protrudes a two-edged sword. While the sword speaks of sharp and cutting judgment, that double rainbow promises peace. Dürer sees good news and not cold justice alone as Christ's deepest intention. Many interpreters have had a difficult time seeing any rainbows in Revelation. The sword is easy to find.

John (but not Dürer) describes Christ as holding in his grasp "the keys of Death and Hades" (1:18). That portrait is essential for all that John has to say. He summons his readers to resist the Roman way of life. He knows that such resistance is perilous. It had cost Jesus his life at the hands of Pontius Pilate. But God raised Jesus from the dead. John pictures him triumphant over death and promising resurrection to his faithful followers, holding aloft the keys that unlock the gates of death and open wide the doors of the kingdom of God to all the faithful (Matthew 16:18-19).

Dürer represents Christ's power differently. He knew perfectly well how to picture keys, as the last of the cuts (number 15) demonstrates so clearly. But here Dürer chooses to portray Christ not with huge iron keys but instead with a great open Book. What

Dürer is doing here is indicating that Death and Hades can be overpowered by the might of Christ's word. Death and Hades are tightening their grip on the Seven Churches, just as the emperor holds the Seer in his grasp. But Christ writes to the Seven Churches through the Seer in order to set them free from their fear of Rome, their fear of being different, their fear of ridicule, ostracism, or even persecution, their fear of taking up the Cross and following Jesus, their fear of Death and Hades.

God's Book and the Empire's Swords

In his opening woodcut Dürer has pictured one of earth's mighty emperors surrounded by a whole arsenal of weapons: swords, spears, lances, and boiling oil. Christ's weaponry is altogether different. Dürer pictures Christ holding in his left hand a great Book. That Book is not in the text of Revelation, but Dürer captures John's intent perfectly, and he telegraphs his meaning with an artistic flourish all his own. He carefully draws the sword proceeding from Christ's mouth so that it touches the upper edges of the Book. That touch seems to me to be significant. I think that Dürer is saying that the two-edged power of Christ and the breath of Christ are in "this book."

The Apocalypse is the sword of Christ's mouth, and the churches will live or die, conquer or be conquered, depending on their response to his message of God's sovereign rule, of Rome's relentless pressuring, and of the churches' need to resist in faith.

John and Dürer describe Christ as the Leader of the forces of God in a Holy War against the injustice and oppressions of the empire. Christ has a "sword," but his "sword" is a Book, a Word, a Revelation, an unveiling of the truth about earth and heaven, about the kingdom of God and the empire of Rome. The sword has two sharp edges, so God's Word both threatens and promises.

By beginning with these two woodcuts, one of Domitian and the other of Christ, Dürer is contrasting two kinds of emperor and two kinds of weapon. It's Domitian against Christ, earth versus heaven, darkness versus light, evil versus good. In the long run all the weaponry of the emperor of earth will prove to be impotent and vain. And the Word of Christ, which appears at times to be so pathetically weak, will finally be seen to be mighty and immortal. Maybe that is why a sword lies useless on the pavement in front of the emperor in the first woodcut, while another sword floats in the air like a living word issuing from the mouth of Christ in woodcut 2. In fact, Dürer seems

fascinated with swords-as-words and draws them into numerous scenes, even where the text of Revelation says nothing about them (as in woodcuts number 6, 8, 11, 12).

Seven Letters to Seven Churches *(2:1–3:22)*

It seems as though that sharp two-edged sword issuing from Christ's mouth in Dürer's woodcut should stab directly at the emperor. Instead it pokes at one of the seven lampstands. To make sure we understand the imagery, John tells us that the seven lampstands are the Seven Churches (1:12, 20). Dürer captures John's intent: Christ's sword, his word, stabs at the churches. We might wish that the book of Revelation were a comforting word for the churches and a tough word for the world. But Revelation is a sharp word addressed to seven particular churches of ancient Asia Minor and to all the churches of yesterday and today.

The Artist coaxes our eyes downward from the mouth of Christ along that sword to the first lampstand, then clockwise around the circle of lamps, and finally up to the extended right hand holding seven stars, which are the seven angels of the Seven Churches (1:16-20). For good or ill, Christ is enthroned in the midst of the churches. And the seven stars, the great and powerful guardian angels of the Seven Churches, are all held fast in Christ's unyielding grip.

Christ commands the Seer, "Write!" (1:19) to the Seven Churches. The imperative "Write!" is repeated seven times in chapters 2 and 3, at the beginning of each of the seven letters. And Christ does not tell the Seer to write whatever he wishes. He tells the Seer to take dictation.

The Seven Churches are real places known to the Seer and named by him. They are the churches of Ephesus, Smyrna, Pergamum, Thyatira, Sardis, Philadelphia, and Laodicea (1:11). The seven letters or edicts dictated by Christ and sent by John (Rev 2–3) are tailored to the situations of each of the Seven Churches.

Each begins with a title for Christ echoing some piece of John's inaugural vision (see 2:1, 8, 12, 18; 3:1, 7, 14). Then the body of each letter contains a brief unveiling of the church introduced by "I know," reminding the readers that they live under the eye of the all-seeing Christ. Then follow sections of praise and blame. Smyrna and Philadelphia are not called to repentance, and Laodicea receives no praise. The letters to the other four churches are a mix of praise and blame. All seven letters conclude with a call to "listen" and with the promise that the "victors" in God's Holy War will receive precious gifts of life.

Fundamentalists and the Letters

Fundamentalist interpreters of the letters stress the prophetic character of the letters and see them as predictions of seven stages in church history: (1) Ephesus = the apostolic church (A.D. 30–100), (2) Smyrna = the persecuted church (A.D. 100–312), (3) Pergamum = the church getting comfortable in the world after the conversion of Constantine (A.D. 312–600), (4) Thyatira = the church of the papacy with its priests and rituals and sacraments (600 until the tribulation), (5) Sardis = the churches of the Reformation which started well but then retained infant baptism and ritualism and developed into state churches (1517 until the tribulation), (6) Philadelphia = the faithful church bearing clear witness to God in its doctrines (the modern missionary movement 1750 until the rapture), and (7) Laodicea = the lukewarm mainline churches of the semi-pagan ecumenical movement (A.D. 1900 until the tribulation).

Liberationist Reading of the Letters

Liberationists stress the language of political and economic struggle as they interpret the seven letters. They believe that rich and powerful Christians, then and now, offer a watered down version of Christianity. They spiritualize the faith, so that they can participate freely and fully in the political, economic, and social life of the dominant culture. They should instead commit themselves to the task of building God's reign (kingdom) in the world, and that means constituting an alternative human community of justice in opposition to the prevailing system of domination. But instead they teach that God's reign is heavenly and other-worldly or inner and spiritual, so emptying it of any power to effect earthly change.

In this liberationist view the letters declare not that Christ's second coming is about to happen and that his coming will solve the problem of oppression by defeating it in the future "battle of Armageddon." Liberationists emphasize instead that Christ is always coming to the churches, strengthening them to oppose the oppressive system in the hope of bringing it down.

The Letters and the Mainline

With most mainline interpreters, I view with great skepticism the fundamentalist scheme of seven ages of the church popularized by the Scofield Bible and many television evangelists. I find it hard to imagine that John was trying to stir up the poor in the Seven Churches so that they would mount public protests against the economic, political, and religious policies of the Roman Empire. Liberationists do, however, offer a healthy and necessary reminder that disciples of Jesus Christ are called in our own time to exercise not simply passive patience but active resistance, not mere sympathy for the oppressed but gutsy solidarity.

The seven letters are a window into the Christian world of the late first century. When we look through them, we see that Christian leaders were not all agreed on what stance the churches, as communities of faith, should adopt toward the larger society.

In John's view, the Seven Churches were being led astray by Christian leaders whom John calls "false apostles" (2:2). John does not use their own Christian names when he refers to them but contemptuously calls them "Nicolaitans" (2:6, 15), followers of "Balaam" (2:14) and "Jezebel" (2:20). John says that they teach the churches what he describes sarcastically as "the deep things of Satan" (2:24). They may have called their teaching "the deep things of God" or something of that sort.

John says that these other Christian leaders encourage the churches to eat meat sacrificed to idols and to practice immorality and fornication (2:14, 20, 24). Like "eating forbidden fruit" or "being in bed with the enemy," those phrases are old metaphors for blurring the line between the sacred and the secular, for underestimating the power of demons and idols, for worshiping false gods. From John's point of view, that's what the teachings of his Christian opponents amounted to.

Christ and Culture

John feared that the Seven Churches were yielding to the temptation to adopt the values of the dominant culture of the Roman Empire. They were conforming to ordinary Roman ways instead of practicing resistance. Other Christian leaders in the Seven Churches evaluated the culture more positively than John. Instead of sharp words of prophetic criticism, they taught that it was perfectly possible to be both good citizens of Roman society and faithful members of the new Christian communities. They probably regarded John as unnecessarily cranky, nasty, and negative.

I confess that I find it troubling that the Seer speaks so harshly of Christian brothers and sisters who disagree with him. Did his rivals really deserve the names "Balaam" and "Jezebel"? Did they teach anything more shocking than what we read in 1 Pet 2:17, that Christians should "honor the emperor"? Or anything more terrible than what we see in 1 Tim 2:1-2, that Christians should pray for "kings and all who hold high office"? I wonder what the authors of 1 Peter, 1 Timothy, and Revelation would have to say to one another, if they all sat down around a table and talked about the life of Christian communities in the midst of a largely non-Christian culture.

The Seer reveals detailed knowledge of the historical and spiritual circumstances of each individual church. The letters seem firmly embedded in an ancient time and place. But these seven letters are a challenge not only to seven ancient churches. They raise questions for our own lives. Easy accommodation by the church to the dominant culture is not only a first-century issue. It is a perennial issue for the Christian community.

Back in 1951 H. Richard Niebuhr wrote an influential book called *Christ and Culture*. In it he set forth some typical Christian answers to the question of how the churches have understood their relationship to the larger culture under the following provocative chapter headings: Christ Against Culture, The Christ of Culture, Christ Above Culture, Christ and Culture in Paradox, Christ and the Transformation of Culture. Clearly the author of Revelation believed that Christ was against the ancient culture, and he also thought that other Christian leaders of his day preferred a Christ of culture. Niebuhr wrote his book as a contribution to "the mutual understanding of variant and often conflicting Christian groups." By contrast the Seer was a single-minded prophet, tossing out his words like thunderbolts, seeking obedience and not conversation.

"Seven" is the number of fullness or completeness, and so these Seven Churches are a representation of the whole church in John's time and place. And they also compel us to think of the whole church in our own time and place. The Seer's words live on, and, like them

or not, they call us to self-examination as surely as if they were written yesterday.

Receiving Revelation

Dürer pictures a youthful John, hands folded in prayer, kneeling at the feet of the exalted Christ. Those folded hands are a Dürer trademark. But more important than those hands are the clothing of Christ and John. The triumphant Christ, seated on the rainbow, is dressed more simply than the emperor in Dürer's first woodcut. And in contrast to all those marvelously costumed citizens and courtiers of the preceding woodcut, John is shown here in a simple white robe. John is dressed just like the saints in woodcuts 5 and 13. In every society, clothing is a signal of job or status. The Seer is calling all readers, whatever their vocation or position, to aspire above all to be clothed simply in fidelity to God.

In Dürer's woodcut John wears neither shoes nor sandals but kneels barefoot before Christ, like Moses before the burning bush (Exod 3:5). To be in the divine presence, whether on Patmos or Sinai or in any other geography, is to stand on holy ground.

Dürer pictures John resting his knees not on the solid earthy rock of Patmos but on a cloud. In the text of Revelation he falls on his face like a dead man (1:17). Icons of the Byzantine tradition regularly picture John asleep or entranced, lying on his back with his right hand extended, palm open toward heaven, like every good disciple ready to receive God's revelation. Dürer here offers his own portrait of an awed and grateful writer who is first of all a faithful Listener and Seer. What does he hear, and what does he see?

Chapter 5

Revelation 4:1–5:14

Heaven's Throne Room

John now reports a second vision. His first occurred on earth, on the island of Patmos (1:9-20), and appropriately enough it was a vision of Jesus Christ who lived on the earth, was buried in the earth, and was raised up to new life from his earthly tomb. In his life and death and resurrection he was and is "God with us."

But now John is caught up from earth to heaven and sees "a throne and One seated on the throne" (4:1-2). God enthroned, God as "the Lord God Almighty," God worshiped by the entire cosmos, is the central vision and guiding conviction of the Seer throughout the book of Revelation. God and no other is worthy of our worship and praise (4:3-11).

The One seated on the throne holds a mysterious scroll, sealed with seven seals, and the call goes out, "Who is worthy to open the scroll?" The Christ of the first vision is then introduced into the second. John watches as the Lamb, once slaughtered but now alive forever, takes from God's hand the seven-sealed scroll (5:7). At that, the four living creatures, the twenty-four elders, and myriads of angels fill the cosmos with songs praising God and the Lamb (5:8-14).

The third of Dürer's woodcuts, marvelously detailed, captures almost everything in John's narration of events in heaven's throne room.

Heaven's Throne Room
(Rev 4:1–5:14)

One Seated on a Throne (4:1-7)

Chapters 4 and 5 of Revelation describe a drama unfolding by stages, but Dürer has managed to seize everything at once and crowd it all into a single blazing moment. In his woodcut, the entire heavenly scene, crammed with creatures and angels and elders, is framed by huge wooden panels. The door of heaven is no longer barred and bolted. It has been flung wide open on its great hinges (4:1), just as the heavens were torn apart at Jesus' baptism (Mark 1:10). John the Seer kneels front and center. He has been transported upward in spirit (as in 1:10) through that opened door, and one of the elders explains to him all that he is seeing and hearing in the heavenly throne room, the eternal holy of holies.

Everything in the Seer's text is packed into the Artist's picture: God sits on a great throne and stares straight ahead, while a rainbow or nimbus shimmers all around. In fact, Dürer's God seems to preside in motionless serenity at the eye of some heavenly storm. Everything else moves in an expanding series of concentric circles around God's throne.

Floating above the throne are seven fiery torches, which the Seer interprets as the seven spirits of God (4:5). They are the seven angels of the presence, always ready to carry God's word from heaven's throne to the farthest corner of creation (cf. 1:4; 3:1; 8:2). Close to the throne on left and right, the four living creatures flap their wings and join the celestial song. Ringing the throne farther out are the twenty-four elders (representing the twelve tribes of Israel and the twelve apostles, working together as a heavenly council) with their individual carved wooden thrones, some casting down their golden crowns, others busily strumming their harps, all of them raising anthems to God and to the Lamb.

The prophet Ezekiel once had a vision of God's throne and of four living creatures (Ezek 1:5-24). In Ezekiel each of the four creatures has four faces, and so each is simultaneously like a lion, an ox, an eagle, and a human. In Revelation, however, one of the four living creatures is like a Lion, the second is like an Ox, the third has a face like a Human Being, and the fourth is like a flying Eagle (4:6-7). Originally they may have represented wild and domesticated animals (Lion and Ox), the birds of the air (Eagle), and the whole life of women and men (Human). In the Bible these four creatures are cherubim, angelic representatives of the entire cosmos of living beings, offering up their ceaseless praise to God their Creator.

Since earliest Christian times, the four living creatures have been associated more narrowly with the four evangelists. Matthew (Human), Mark (Lion), Luke (Ox), and John (Eagle) bear witness in their varying idioms and voices to the one Christ of God.

Holy, Holy, Holy (4:8-11)

As John describes them, the four living creatures are awesome and terrible guardians of God's throne. They have six wings, they are full of eyes, and they cry, "Holy, Holy, Holy," day and night without end (4:8; see Isa 6:2-3). Besides supporting the celestial chants in praise of God, their task is to bar the approach of anything or anyone unclean or unworthy. In Dürer's crowded picture the four creatures seem like unimpressive household pets flitting about nervously in the throne room of God. They seem no fiercer than the terrier lying at Domitian's feet in the first of the woodcuts.

Earth may defy God with idolatry, immorality, or idle indifference. But the four living creatures and the twenty-four elders and the myriads of the angels of heaven praise God without ceasing: "You are worthy, our Lord and God, to receive glory and honor . . . , for you created all things" (4:11). The challenge of the Seer's glowing vision is for the readers to praise God on earth as God is praised by all the inhabitants of heaven. ("Your will be done on earth as it is in heaven!") And the promise (and perhaps also the threat!) is that the way things are in heaven now is the way they will be on earth in the end. Emperors like Domitian may oppress God's people for a brief passing hour, and cities like Rome may exalt themselves over tribes and tongues and multitudes for hundreds of years, and even people in the churches may be swayed to adore emperors and idolize political and economic systems, but they need to know that God will finally reign over a new heaven and a new earth, and of God's reign there will be no end. The promise of the entire New Testament is that the new politics of God, enfleshed in Jesus, will replace the tired old politics of domination practiced by rulers on earth through the centuries.

A Scroll Sealed with Seven Seals (5:1-5)

As the fifth chapter of Revelation opens, the Seer notes for the first time that God's hand grips a mysterious scroll, full of writing front and back, inside and out (cf. Exod 32:15; Ezek 2:10). It is brimming with revelation for humankind. But the scroll is sealed not with one seal but with seven seals and cannot be opened. Dürer portrays God's feet as resting on the back of a mighty angel who cries out, "Who is worthy to break the seals and open this scroll?" (5:2). At first no one steps forward to answer the call. The Seer begins to weep. How incredibly sad if the deepest secrets of the universe, the designs of God's heart, should remain locked and sealed up.

However, one of the elders reassures the Seer: "The Lion of the tribe of Judah has gained the victory" (5:5), and so he is worthy to break the seals and open the scroll. Out of all the beings in the universe, the Lion of Judah alone is worthy to enter the dangerously charged innermost circle of light and approach the throne of God.

The Lion-Lamb (5:6-8)

Hearing that announcement, John turns to look. He expects to see a Lion, but strangely he sees not a Lion but a Lamb. And he describes the Lamb in a paradox: the Lamb has been slaughtered and yet it is standing fully alive again and triumphant (5:6). This language means that the Lion-Lamb is the crucified and resurrected Jesus, who died and yet lives forever (1:18).

What is going on here? Many believe that this vision serves to correct the old nationalistic and militant tradition which expected the Messiah to be a Lion, conquering the enemies of God's people. John's vision would then signal that the hoped for Lion has turned out to be more of a Lamb. In many passages of the New Testament it is certainly true that the Messiah rescues by pouring out his life in a torrent of suffering love and not by rending and tearing in the manner of traditional warriors. So the vision may de-

clare that the Messiah "conquers" but not in the manner of earthbound kings and generals.

But perhaps the vision works the other way around. It seems very likely that the Seer is solemnly reminding his readers that the Christ, the Lamb of God, is also the mighty Lion of Judah. They were forgetting the power and majesty of the Lamb. To say that the Lamb is the Lion is a wake-up call, summoning us readers to take Christ's holy will and his mighty judgment with the utmost seriousness.

The Lamb of Revelation is certainly no weakling. The power of the Lamb and even the "wrath" of the Lamb (6:16-17) are the Seer's theme from start to finish. The Lamb is a great and awesome figure in Revelation, once slaughtered but now alive in the presence of almighty God. The Lamb will gain full victory over all God's enemies (17:14). He will be enthroned with God in the New Jerusalem (22:1-3) and will forever shepherd the people of God (7:17).

Dürer's Lamb is unfortunately one of his least successful drawings. His Lamb seems too anemic for the great tasks assigned to it by the Seer. Nevertheless Dürer follows the Seer in picturing the Lamb (5:6) as having seven horns (= full and universal power) and seven eyes (= fullest, deepest wisdom and knowledge) (5:6).

As long as the scroll in God's right hand stays sealed, everyone waits in suspense. No book can reveal its contents as long as it stays closed. A will does not and cannot become effective until it is opened. Only then do its provisions begin to go into effect.

Worthy the Lamb! (5:9-14)

As the Lamb takes the book from the hand of God, the four living creatures and the twenty-four elders break into an anthem of praise. Together they sing, "You are worthy!" (5:9).

Their song is called a "new" song (5:9; 14:3; 15:3-4; Ps 33; 3). But why "new"? Why not call it angelic or astonishing, melodic, or enchanting? Why not moving or passionate? Why "new"? The book of Revelation announces that God is about to do a new thing. "New" is the quality of the "new heaven and new earth" in contrast to the "first heaven and the first earth" which will soon pass away (21:1). "New" describes the "new Jerusalem" (21:2), also called the "holy" city (12:10). "New" means a cosmos purged of all that is idolatrous and twisted and unclean. "New" is the opposite of unjust, oppressive, exploitative, uncaring, demonic. God will finally sweep away the "old" and bring into being a new world, shouting for all to hear, "See! I am making all things new" (21:5).

The song of the creatures and elders is "new" because it celebrates the new world which God reveals and creates beginning with the martyr death and glorious resurrection of Jesus. God's new beginning in the Lion-Lamb is like the creation out of darkness in the beginning, like the exodus from slavery in Egypt, like the great homecoming from exile in Babylon. The Human who was a Lion, by dying like a sacrificial Ox and soaring up like an Eagle, has gained for God a new and universal people from every tribe and tongue and people and nation (5:9; 7:9; 11:4; 13:7; 14:6; Dan 7:14). The newness of that fellowship consists not only in their universality but in the fact that they are a community which finally incarnates God's sovereign rule, serving God as holy priests (1:5-6; 5:10).

Then the Seer hears the voices of angels, myriads of myriads, tens of thousands times tens of thousands, joining the praise and singing, "To the one seated on the throne and to the Lamb be blessing and honor and glory and might forever and ever!" (5:13). And the living creatures roar and bellow and shriek and shout their "Amen!" (5:14).

Dürer's Throne Room

Dürer's Lamb stands on its hind legs with forepaws solidly planted on the Book. The mysterious Book, sealed with its seven seals, lies freshly opened on the lap of God, who alone of all the many figures in the agitated scene is all serenity. God stares out of the woodcut as though interrogating and warning us readers.

In each of his first three woodcuts Dürer pictures an exalted figure seated on a throne. The image of the throne or the idea of sovereignty is absolutely central to the book of Revelation. Whose world is this? Whose will or command should shape our lives in the world? To whom do we owe our existence and our allegiance? These questions are far from academic. The opening woodcuts like the opening chapters of Revelation reveal a sharp conflict between powers, and that conflict spills over into the churches, where men and women differ in their earnest responses to the power of God on the one hand and to the power of the political and social systems in which they live on the other. In our present setting, what does it mean to pray, "Your name be hallowed; your kingdom come; your will be done on earth as in heaven"?

The Earth Below

Dürer's third woodcut pictures not only the scene in heaven's throne room but also the world below, even though the Seer himself offers not even a single word about the earth at this point in the text of Revelation.

When Dürer pictures earth, we might expect him to draw scenes of insolence or immorality or of imperial troops extorting taxes or compelling sacrifice to the emperor or of the rich and powerful grinding the faces of the poor into the dust of the earth. Instead Dürer shows us the world as a city at peace, slumbering behind its moat, protected by its turrets, enjoying the fruits of the earth and the goods carried by seagoing vessels.

Dürer's city is completely unaware of events in heaven. But look at those flames leaping from heaven and piercing the clouds, flashing downward toward an unsuspecting world. A pair of heads representing destructive winds (see woodcut 6) not only peer earthward but begin to blow. Others are seen high above the throne of God, and they also have begun to fill their cheeks. Terrible storms are brewing. The seals are about to be broken. The Lamb is ready to unmask the injustices and cruelties of human societies and to unveil also the heart and mind of God.

What will the breaking of the seals mean for the church and for the world? What will it take to get the attention of the church and of the world? What is the divine strategy for winning earth to the praise of the God of justice and love?

Chapter 6

Revelation 6:1-8

The Four Horsemen

As the Lamb breaks each of the first four of the seven seals, one of the living creatures cries out, "Go!" and, one after the other, the famed Four Horsemen of the Apocalypse begin their terrible ride (6:1-8). What's happening here? I had expected that the scroll, full of writing inside and out, would reveal to us the depths of the compassion of God. And the Lamb's breaking of the seals should set in motion the loving purposes of God. But breaking the seals summons the Four Horsemen, and their riding is bad news, not good news.

In the fourth of his woodcuts Dürer gives us so much to look at that we almost forget that the four horses of John's Revelation are snow white and blood red, midnight black and ghastly green. Dürer's horses are so real, so marvelously sculpted, that we can almost see their colors and hear their terrible hoofbeats and their snorting, and we feel their movement. But what do they mean, and how can we understand their awful ride?

The Four Horsemen
(Rev 6:1-8)

The Lamb breaks the first four seals of the scroll, and Dürer pictures four horsemen galloping forth, neck and neck, a deadly phalanx racing across the sky and downward upon the earth. In Dürer's woodcut the horsemen are neither monsters nor cartoon characters. They are human beings of flesh and blood, the Artists' own contemporaries.

The book of Revelation describes the first two riders as mounted Parthian (Persian) warriors, always threatening Rome's eastern frontiers. Fear of Parthian invasion sent shudders down the spines of Roman citizens in John's day, but in Dürer's time it was the Turks who threatened Europe. So Dürer's first two riders wear the beards and headdress of the feared Turkish warriors who were pressing hard against the eastern borders of Europe in the late-fifteenth century.

At the top of the woodcut the first rider, outfitted like a crowned prince, takes deadly aim at some doomed target of his dreaded bow. His horse is white, the color of victory (6:2). He is followed closely by the second rider, a heartless warrior swinging a terrible swift sword. We have seen imperial and celestial swords in woodcuts 1 and 2, and we will see swords frequently again in Dürer's woodcuts, even when they are not mentioned in the Seer's text. This second horseman rides a red horse, the color of blood and of the slaughter inevitable in warfare (6:4).

The third horseman is no armed warrior like the first two. Dürer pictures him as a smug banker or wealthy tax collector or perhaps a pawn broker. He is all decked out in fancy jacket and expensive necklace, his ample middle held in by a great belt. He sits on a tooled leather saddle, and his feet are stuck in ornamental stirrups. He raises his arm and swings his scales like a weapon against the poor. This rider brings a punishing scarcity, but he experiences none of it himself. He raises to exorbitant levels the price of wheat and barley, staples of the peasant diet, but he leaves unchanged the price of wine and oil (6:6). In the Seer's mind this third rider is famine, the inevitable result of the ravages of war represented by the first two riders.

Bringing up the rear, both in John's text and in Dürer's woodcut, is the fourth rider, bearing the grim name of "Death" or "Plague." His horse is ghastly green, the color of decomposing corpses. Dürer pictures this fourth horseman as a gruesome Father Time, raking people with his pitchfork into the monstrous jaws of Hades (6:8), clearly seen in the lower left hand corner.

Dürer carefully differentiates these four riders. In his composition the third rider holds center stage. Not only does he fill the precise center of the woodcut, but he is also drawn on a larger scale than his three companions. Furthermore, we see his full figure, from the top of his head to the very tip of his slippered toes. Dürer fixes our attention especially on this rider who brings a crushing scarcity to human life. In Dürer's day usury and taxes were an enormous burden, producing terrible economic pressure, even crushing the peasantry and ordinary folk. In every economy and also in our own some people amass obscene fortunes while others can barely eke out a living. Are poverty and unemployment and homelessness inevitable? They are terrible realities in every human society, but they will form no part of God's New Jerusalem.

All four riders bring death. And the Seer has in mind not just what we call death by natural causes but unnatural and especially painful forms of death: by sword, by famine, by pestilence, and by wild beasts (6:8).

Trampled

It is worth contemplating the faces of the victims of the Four Horsemen in Dürer's woodcut. We see a housewife with sewing kit fixed to her waist, a well-fed burgher with chubby jowls, a peasant staring uncomprehendingly at his impending fate, a bald-pated monk face down on the earth, utterly defeated. They are ordinary, believable citizens, no more evil than their neighbors.

Some classes or strata of society because of their piety or money or influence at court may imagine that they can stave off the ills and misfortunes that befall frail human beings. But in Dürer's woodcut, the first to go into Hades' all-devouring and greedy mouth is a cardinal in fancy hat. That tempts us to think that Dürer, working in the early dawn of Reformation times, is indulging in a piece of anti-clerical polemic. But what we have here is a common theme in medieval representations of the Last Judgment and in portrayals of the Dance of Death. In harmony with that late medieval tradition, Dürer teaches that death finally makes equals of us all, including the most powerful and the most highly privileged.

Misfortune can strike with terrible speed, and finally death bears us all away. Dürer reminds us of the universal human fate and summons us to readiness.

Who Are These Horsemen?

The Four Horsemen pose a hard question. How can these terrifying riders be the result when the Lamb begins to break the seals on the mysterious book? Doesn't the Book contain God's good and gracious will for humankind? Isn't God a God of grace and mercy and promise? How can catastrophe be the first word out of God's Book? What do these Horsemen signify?

Fundamentalist Thought

In fundamentalist interpretation, most of Revelation (chapters 4–19) refers to the final seven years of planet earth. The opening of the seven seals offers a chronological sketch of the major events of that final seven-year period, called The Tribulation.

We still live today in the time of grace. Fundamentalists believe that this time will be concluded by the Rapture, when all faithful Christians will be lifted bodily to heaven. After the Rapture, other events of the end time will follow swiftly. Many Jews (144,000) will be converted (Rev 7:1-7), and they will be missionaries leading countless Gentiles to faith (Rev 7:8-17). Satan will summon up Antichrist and make war against Israel and these converts. God will break forth in judgment and begin to settle accounts. These final years of planet earth are sometimes called in Scripture "the Day of the Lord" and sometimes "the Tribulation." The final 3½ years of that last seven-year period will be "the Great Tribulation."

So fundamentalists stress that John in his Revelation is not describing events which punctuate all of human history but is predicting in detailed fashion events of the final days of planet earth after the Rapture, after the departure of true Christians from the earth, immediately before the Second Coming of Christ. The Four Horsemen represent the sudden outburst of God's definitive wrath upon a sinful world.

Liberationist Interpretation

Various liberationists see the Four Horsemen as representing four destructive aspects of the Roman Empire. Rome rides high over the peoples of the earth (1) with its victorious wars, (2) its political violence, (3) its oppressive economic policies, and (4) it brings nothing but death and destruction. Repeatedly in human history, empires and governments have held out bright promises of peace and prosperity, achieving those goals for some few citizens, but all too often at enormous human cost, leaving in their wake a trail of bloodshed, poverty, and death.

Alternately, some liberationists see in the Four Horsemen the sign that the Roman Empire, which bragged of its power and its longevity ("eternal Rome"), was itself about to be overrun and brought to ruin.

In liberationist reading, the fifth seal (souls under the altar, Rev 6:9-11) indicates that Rome arouses in heaven the impassioned outcry of martyrs for justice and vengeance. They beg God to destroy the oppressive Roman system. They are told they must wait while God offers the world an opportunity to repent. For a short time more martyrdoms will occur, but God's wrath will erupt against oppressors when the sixth seal is broken (6:12-17). The good news is that the people of God, marked with the seal of God, will be saved.

So in liberationist thinking, the seven seals are encouragement to martyrs and potential martyrs in every age of the church, summoning them to exert themselves in the building of an alternative community. We must resist the oppressive powers of our time and place. Being sealed (7:1-12) means more than being baptized or holding membership. It means acting in history to bring about the downfall of the evil empire. Christians press on with their efforts, inspired by the vision of a utopian future of God's just empire on earth (7:13-17).

With the Mainline

Mainline interpreters stress that these horsemen, these destructive powers in human history, cannot be understood nor can they be endured when they are viewed in isolation. Both the Seer and the Artist insist that these four horsemen are not God's last word. Disasters, catastrophes, evils, and even death are all temporary and preliminary. They may appear to be invincible, crushing humanity underfoot, and yet their powers are strictly limited to the time before the end.

Bursting from some hidden starting gate, Dürer's horsemen sweep across the sky in precise formation. They drop out of the heavens like streaks of lightning flashing from the sky, and they plunge wildly from the viewer's left toward the right side of the page. It seems to me that Dürer has deliberately drawn them as racing toward the end of the book. By that device Dürer indicates that the meaning of the horsemen, the meaning of terrors in human history, can be learned only from the perspective of the end. And they can be endured only in view of the end.

Dürer offers a glimpse of his own view of the end and goal of history. He pictures a wonderful angel soaring high above the whole scene of slaughter below. The angel extends both hands, and those hands are carefully drawn to give us two messages. The open left hand touches the terrible sword of the second rider and is a gesture of divine permission for the horsemen to ride forth on their grim mission. But the fingers of the right hand form the familiar sign of blessing. That angel, mighty messenger of God, choreographs the moves of the four horsemen, and keeps them from destroying God's people.

At first it seems that this angel, such an essential element in Dürer's picture, is nowhere to be found in the Seer's text. However, that angelic face, with its mysterious and enigmatic smile, represents not only Dürer's faith but John's own. One of John's chief goals is to remove the veil from historical events and enable us to see at least for a moment the transcendent reality behind and beyond the visible. Both the Seer and the Artist assure us that God has not lost control over history, even when disasters strike.

As John tells the story, the Lamb snaps the seals on the mysterious scroll, one after the other. As each of the first four seals is broken, one of the Four Living Creatures cries out, "Go!" Only when that signal comes from the throne do the riders plunge forth in rapid succession. Mysteriously, they move out only when they are commanded, and the catastrophes which they represent are all under divine control.

According to John and Dürer, God's presence and blessing go with the faithful, even into the valley of the shadow of death. Night and terror, dreadful realities which regularly invade human lives, are not God's final word. The strong wings of this guiding and guarding angel extend their reach over all the terrors of the scene, just as God's people are borne up on eagle's wings (Rev 12:14), or as a mother hen gathers her chicks beneath her wings (Luke 13:34; Ps 17:8).

John and Jesus

The pounding hoofbeats of the Four Horsemen of the Apocalypse echo words spoken by Jesus on the eve of his death. In the so-called "Little Apocalypse" (Mark 13 with parallels in Matthew 24–25 and Luke 21) Jesus solemnly reviews the history of the church and the world in the days before the ultimate triumph of God. He names trials to be endured before the end. The lists of coming trials differ slightly in the three evangelists. Common to their reports are these three: wars, earthquakes, and famines. Luke has pestilence as a fourth disaster (Luke 21:10-11; cf. Mark 13:8; Matt 24:7).

Those four coming storms foreseen by Jesus (wars, earthquakes, famines, pestilence) sound very much like the Four Horsemen of Revelation 6. Both Jesus in the Gospels and John in his Revelation declare that these catastrophes are not God's last word on a fallen creation.

It is crucial to note that the Four Horsemen represent not the totality of the present or future but only the beginning in a series of seven events. We will see immediately that their riding provokes the cry of the saints (the fifth seal, 6:7-11), which then moves God to act (the sixth seal, 6:12-17). What is their cry, and what is God's response? And what happens with the breaking of the seventh seal?

Chapter 7

Revelation 6:9-17

Opening the Fifth and Sixth Seals

At the snapping of the fifth seal, John sees righteous souls in heaven beneath the altar of God, crying out, "How long, Lord?" (6:9-10). How long will it be before heaven acts to vindicate God's faithful servants? Then, at the breaking of the sixth seal, John witnesses earthquakes below and chaos in the heavens above, as the long-expected day of God's wrath, the day for which the righteous souls cried out, begins to dawn (6:12-13).

The upper third of Dürer's fifth woodcut follows one of the souls beneath the altar in a kind of "martyr's progress." The woodcut in its entirety manages to capture most of what John describes as happening with the breaking of the fifth and sixth seals.

Opening the Fifth and Sixth Seals
(Rev 6:9-17)

The Fifth Seal *(6:9-11)*

At the breaking of the fifth seal John sees the heavenly altar and beneath it the souls martyred for their faithful witness to the word of God. And he hears those souls cry out, "Lord and Master, holy and true, how long must we wait before you judge and avenge our blood?" (6:10).

The divine response is almost heartbreaking. Those saints each receive a fresh white robe, symbol of victory and of intimacy with God. And then they are told that they must wait. God's final triumph is not yet. It is coming soon, but the struggle goes on and more martyrdoms must occur before the end.

A Dramatic Cycle in Dürer's Woodcut

Above the clouds in the upper third of Dürer's print, we see the martyred souls, both male and female, young and old, all stacked up like cordwood beneath the heavenly altar. They all lie there naked and unmoving in postures of death.

But we see one bearded figure moving through an intriguing cycle, and Dürer invites us to follow his progress. At first we see this bearded martyr sleeping the sleep of death with fellow martyrs immediately beneath the altar in the upper left of the woodcut. Then above the three sleeping figures we see an angel tenderly rousing this one martyr from his mortal slumbers. The angel grips the martyr's left wrist, pulls him up out of death and points towards a stack of white robes lying ready on the altar. On the far side of the altar we see the same fellow reaching up to take his robe from the angel's helping hand. At the extreme right side of the circle of angels and robing figures, the same solicitous angel helps the martyr climb into his new garment. Finally he turns, and on his knees he faces the altar, now fully robed, among other robed figures.

At the base of the altar Dürer pictures a circle of three robed figures lost in deep discussion with one another. What are they talking about? The meaning of the lives they have lived and the wonders, long hidden, which they now at last enjoy? Perhaps they are inquiring of one another and of God, "How long?" How long must the present terrors continue? How long will evil and injustice roam the earth unchecked by the righteousness of heaven? How long before churches on earth shake off their lukewarmness and begin to confront oppressors and stand solidly with victims? How long before God intervenes and renders divine judgment? "How long, O Lord?" (6:10).

The full-faced figure with robe secured at the throat by a clasp, palm extended upwards, is an angel offering heavenly explanations to the saints. The two figures pictured in profile look exactly like the Seer himself in face, posture, and dress (see woodcuts 1 and 2).

So the top third of the woodcut is a dramatic cycle to be read in clockwise fashion, beginning with the dead beneath the altar. But that is not all. The man whose destiny we follow at the top of the page is the same figure upon whom stars fall with their burning and crushing weight in the center background of the lower portion of the woodcut. He is raising his left hand. Why is he doing that? Is he trying vainly to ward off those falling stars? I think he is lifting the front of his cap to expose to God's view the seal on his forehead, marking him as one of God's faithful servants. That sealing is described in the following woodcut.

The Sixth Seal *(6:12-17)*

The white robes and offer of rest given to the souls beneath the altar (6:11) are an interim arrangement, an interlude of welcome assurance after the shattering hoofbeats of the Four Horsemen. The snapping of the sixth seal not only returns us to disasters but introduces a grim escalation. The whole earth is shaken, the sun turns as black as sackcloth, the moon becomes like blood, and the stars fall to earth like figs shaken off the tree by a winter storm (6:12-13). Jesus spoke of these same four signs of the approaching end in the days immediately preceding his crucifixion and resurrection (Mark 13:24-25). In Dürer's woodcut, a grimacing sun and a pained moon preside with shocked expressions over a scene of cosmic devastation. Stars fall like great sparks scorching sea and land (cf. 8:10; 9:1; 12:4).

In his vision John sees kings and big shots, colonels and generals, the rich and the powerful, and everyone else both slave and free trying in vain to escape the outpouring of divine judgment. Dürer has people rushing about in a mad effort to find a place to hide. A peasant is sinking into the abyss on the extreme left margin next to a shrieking mother with a young child. On the right, emperor and empress, pope (triple tiara) and cardinal and cowled cleric discover that their tiaras, mitres, crowns, and turbans are no defense against the terrors of the last times. All raise their hands, trying desperately to ward off falling stars. Or are they lifting their hands in gestures of supplication? Some try to burrow into rocks and caves. No more peaceful earth slumbering undisturbed as in woodcut 3!

Day of Wrath *(6:16-17)*

What's going on here? The saints have cried out to God, "Judge and avenge our blood!" (6:10). And now God responds by raining down destruction from heaven. Both the cry and the answer seem heartless. To many readers Revelation seems to picture a church that thirsts for vengeance and a God who answers by throwing a cosmic temper tantrum.

In a terrible phrase, the Seer declares that the people of earth weep and wail at the breaking forth of "the wrath of the Lamb" (6:16). The long awaited Day of the Lord turns out to be a "great day of wrath" (6:17; cf. 11:18; 14:10; 16:19; 19:15).

How can that be? "Wrath" is a hard word. But it is not simply anger or a divine snit. The day of wrath describes the dawn of that day when God begins acting to right every wrong, to overturn every injustice, to call a halt to all oppression. Oppressors experience this "wrath" as divine anger, while the victims of oppression now celebrate the triumph of justice. This awesome day is the answer to their prayer, "Hallowed be your name! Your kingdom come!"

The cosmic shocks of the sixth seal are a kind of divine demolition project, clearing away injustice and all the institutions built on injustice in order to make way for God's New World of righteousness and peace.

Certainly Revelation as a whole does not end with disaster or destruction. John's final vision is of the new Jerusalem descending from God out of heaven as a holy habitation for all nations on a new earth. But when and how will injustice be removed? When and how will the new city be given? Answers differ.

Dürer's Own Response

For his part, Dürer does not answer that question directly. Dürer was personally involved at the beginning of the tumultuous sixteenth century with a circle of artists and intellectuals, priests, and politicians pressing for reform in church and society. Dürer was also on the best of terms with the most powerful figures in his native Germany. Frederick the Wise, Elector of Saxony, was Dürer's patron from 1496. Emperor Maximilian I commissioned work from Dürer and eventually bestowed on him a pension, which was confirmed by the new emperor, Charles V, in 1520. Dürer believed that the New Jerusalem was under construction in the spiritual rebirth of northern Europe, as leaders like Maximilian and Frederick lent their prestige to the reformist programs of Erasmus, Celtis, Melanchthon, and Luther. In the final woodcut in his series on Revelation, the New Jerusalem is not some fantastic, otherworldly metropolis with gates fashioned of huge pearls but is pictured as a scrubbed and tidy German city.

Dürer believed that the whole world would be changed, gradually and steadily, as emperors and archbishops heeded the fresh winds blowing in the northern renaissance.

How Does the Kingdom Come?

Fundamentalists reject Dürer's understanding of the coming of the kingdom. They traditionally hold that the task of the faithful is evangelism. Make converts! Christians are deluding themselves if they imagine they should attempt to cooperate with God in establishing God's kingdom in the world. The world is destined to grow darker and more dangerous, they say. But following the rapture of the true church and the seven-year tribulation, God will give the millennial kingdom and will do so unilaterally.

Nevertheless, it would be a mistake to think that Dürer's reading is out of date. Even now, entering the twenty-first century, many mainline interpreters see in Revelation the promise that God's new world emerges, not just at the end of history but in the midst of history, wherever and whenever the followers of the Lamb practice the love called "agape." That strong love conquers evil. It creates an occasional oasis of compassion in a desert of indifference.

Meanwhile, liberationists contend for a more radical critique of culture on the part of the Christian community. The present political, economic, and social system is so deeply flawed and oppressive that Christians must adopt a stance of active resistance to its blandishments, disdaining its threats. And the community is called to practice a radical solidarity (and not just an inconsequential sympathy) with the poor and marginalized. The churches must stop playing chaplain to the Pentagon and Wall Street, stop sprinkling holy water on tanks and banks. The new Jerusalem, the new society, will arise only as God's faithful people exert themselves strenuously in the public arena.

John's Answer

What is John's own answer to the question of how and when will the new city come? What is John's program? Does he even have what moderns call a program? He certainly has a vision. He foresees the impending collapse of the entire present order of things, and the advent of a totally new heaven and new earth. He believes that his visions will soon become realities, and he therefore heaps scorn on any Christians who slumber through life imagining it is possible to be simultaneously a loyal citizen of the empire and a faithful follower of the Lamb. John believes that the present order is satanic, and he rejoices in advance at its imminent overthrow.

John does not contemplate any human cooperation in the destruction of the present order of things or in the creation of the new world. God will see to its destruction, and God will grant the new cosmos as a fresh act of creation. Human beings are called to stand in awe of God, suffer the pressure of an evil society, and wait for the gift of God's new world. And they should wait for it stubbornly and with supreme confidence. John shames and he scolds, as he summons his readers to repentance and fresh dedication.

Reviewing the Seven Seals

The snapping of the seven seals results in a series of catastrophes falling on the world like hammer blows.

Everything "old" in the sense of fallen, twisted, evil, and corrupt is being broken up. And yet destruction is not the final word. The old world breaks up because the power of God's recreative energy is drawing near, like an approaching storm (Psalm 29). In another context Jesus said, "The heavenly bodies will be shaken." When that happens, he said, "Raise your heads, because your redemption is drawing near" (Luke 21:28). Redemption is coming.

Or in the words of John, the New Jerusalem is coming beyond the destruction of Babylon. God's rule, God's reign, is on the way. Precisely how does it come? How does God establish the "reign of God" or "kingdom of God" in the midst of human life? Does God give the kingdom unilaterally? Or does God enlist human agents? Fundamentalists, evangelicals, more liberal mainline interpreters, and liberationists disagree on the question of the proportions of divine and human activity. But all agree that whenever God's reign erupts in our midst, it shakes the powers. And the promise is that when it comes in all its fullness, it will eclipse and supersede all the monstrosities of earthly and human rule.

Dürer's swirling clouds give his whole composition the shape of an hourglass. Through the narrow neck of clouds, stars fall from the sky like sands in a glass. Thus the Artist graphically reminds us that time is running out. The world is plunging headlong toward its end, and both Seer and Artist want their audiences to know that the end includes God's just judgment. The people of the earth must repent, and that means a fundamental change, while they still have opportunity.

So far both the Seer and the Artist have been busy picturing the terrors of God's judgment. So far only six of the seven seals have been broken. What else will John and Dürer show us before displaying the final triumph of God?

Chapter 8

Revelation 7:1-17

The Seal of the Living God

John has been describing what happens as the seven seals are snapped one after the other. But after six have been broken, the series is interrupted. Between the sixth and seventh seals John reports two visions of two great throngs of people. First he sees 144,000 servants of God, sealed with the seal of the living God (7:1-8). Then John tells of seeing a second multitude, so large that no one could number it (7:9-17).

Who are these two multitudes? Are they two separate and distinct groups? Could they be Jewish-Christians and Gentile-Christians? Or do these two visions describe one and the same people of God but from two different angles?

In a way Dürer has solved the problem. He simply omitted the second of those multitudes! But he has beautifully illustrated the first in the sixth of his woodcuts.

The Seal of the Living God
(Rev 7:1-17)

Dürer draws four strong angels standing in a tight circle, back to back, surrounding a tree laden with fruit. The Seer and the Artist have just described the breaking of the sixth seal and the hard time coming when the storm of the final judgment will break upon the earth. The Seer writes that in that time, stars will fall from the sky like ripe figs shaken from the tree by the last storm of winter (Rev 6:13).

But now, just when we expect the breaking of the seventh and final seal, the Seer describes something entirely different. He reports seeing four angels at the four corners of the earth holding back the four winds (7:1). And he then sees yet another angel bearing "the seal of the living God" and calling to the quartet of strong angels not to harm the earth or the sea or the trees until after God's servants have first been marked with the seal (7:2-3).

Now here is a difficult but important point. In the sequence of the Seer's chapters and in the sequence of the Artist's woodcuts, the sealing of the 144,000 follows the snapping of the first six seals. Yet in narrating the sealing of the servants, both Artist and Seer are describing something that happened before the breaking of the first seal. Before the breaking of the seals (Rev 6), the saints were sealed (Rev 7). Thus they are marked with God's protecting "seal" before the snapping of the terrible "seals."

Four Winds and Four Angels

At the uppermost edge of Dürer's woodcut, an angel bearing a great wooden cross cries out to the four waiting angels, commanding them to hold back the four destructive winds (7:1-3). Exactly as in the Seer's vision, the four angels are both restrained and restraining. With their uplifted hands they signal their obedience to the solemn task of holding back for a moment the destructive winds at the four corners of the earth. The winds are pictured as puffy faces in the clouds, and they do not look particularly threatening. But the four winds and the four angels of Revelation 7 are the same as the Four

Horsemen of Revelation 6. Like the horsemen, the winds and the angels will bring destruction, but not yet.

The four angels stand alert and attentive, their swords at the ready but not yet unleashed (contrast woodcut number 8). In his text John says not a single word about swords. But he does speak of terrible harm coming to earth and sea, to trees and people. Dürer graphically portrays that harm by drawing those awful swords.

In the interval before the four angels begin their dread swordplay, before the four winds begin to blow, before the Four Horsemen begin their fateful gallop, a youthful angel at the lower right corner of the woodcut paints the sign of the cross on the foreheads of a great throng of God's elect kneeling before him.

144,000 *(7:4)*

John describes those sealed by the angel as "one hundred forty-four thousand" (7:4), twelve thousand from each of the twelve tribes of Israel. That all sounds so precise, but who exactly are they? And why are they so carefully numbered?

There were, of course, twelve tribes in old Israel, and Jesus chose twelve disciples as a sign that he was creating a renewed Israel. Jesus once spoke of the twelve disciples sitting on twelve thrones, judging the twelve tribes of Israel (Matt 19:28; Luke 22:30). Even in the days of the New Covenant, "Israel" continued to serve as a name for the totality of the people of God. So Paul could speak of those who trust in Jesus Christ as the "children of Abraham" (Gal 3:29) and as spiritual "Israel" (Gal 6:16).

144,00 is the number 12 squared (= 144) and then multiplied tremendously (144 x 1000 = 144,000). These 12,000 from each tribe remind us that God is faithful to ancient promises stretching all the way from earliest times to the end of history. In their long pilgrimage God's people may suffer terribly and may at times feel totally abandoned, but the exactness and perfection of the number 144,000 is a vivid sign that they are all as carefully numbered and precisely known as the hairs on your head (Matt 10:30). Owned by God, this mighty multitude enjoys God's eternal protection. God has claimed them, and woe betides any who would harm them. The exact number may also be a way of designating the faithful as holy warriors, lined up in their ranks, ready for spiritual warfare.

Dürer has sketched more than a dozen figures in his woodcut. Their robes identify them as noble and peasant, cleric and lay alike. One of the faces looks just like the slave-boy who pours the boiling oil on John in the opening woodcut! The figure kneeling in the foreground with his forehead already marked, gazing upward, may be a self-portrait by Dürer. He looks very much like the man whose story is told in the cycle at the top of the preceding woodcut number 5.

An Angel Bearing God's Seal (7:2)

The angel presiding over the entire scene in Dürer's woodcut is described by John as having ascended "from the rising of the sun" (7:2). That is, this angel comes up from the east, source of all light and hope.

In a description reminiscent of Ezekiel 9, the Seer says that this angel carries "the seal of the living God" (7:2) and uses the seal as a sign of divine protection. The Artist pictures God's seal as a great wooden tau cross slung over the angel's shoulder. And the cross is the mark with which the angel seals the 144,000. It is the sign or seal by which they will endure and even conquer.

Once again it is important to stress that the four winds (7:1) and the four angels (7:1; 9:14) are the same as the Four Horsemen (6:1-8), and woodcuts 4, 5, and 6 should be viewed not as a chronological series but as separate descriptions of the same set of events. They are all images of hurricanes and storms of human history. For purposes of dramatic presentation, the writer of Revelation has first described the terrors. But the Seer wants to assure readers that the terrors of history have no real or lasting power over those who belong to God. With a marvelous play on words the Seer declares that the saints have been "sealed" against the power of the opened "seals." They enjoy divine protection and so can remain faithful even when the bitter winds of trouble and tribulation begin to blow hard.

A Great Multitude (7:9-17)

In addition to the 144,000 the Seer reports a second vision of "a great multitude that no one could count, people from every nation, people out of all tribes and peoples and languages" of earth (7:9). Clothed in saintly white (6:11; 19:8), they stand before the throne of God and of the Lamb. With palm branches in their hands, they sing a song of deliverance (7:10; cf. 14:3; 15:3).

It helps to note that in his vision the Seer himself is asked, "Who exactly are these people robed in white?" (7:13). He confesses ignorance. Then one of the elders tells the Seer that this multitude has passed triumphantly through "the great ordeal" (7:14 NRSV; NIV follows KJV in using the phrase "the great tribulation"; see 1:9; 3:10; 13:5-10). They have "made their robes white by washing them in the blood of the Lamb." How can the stain of red blood turn robes sparkling white? The blood of this Lamb is a cleansing flood! (see 1:5) They followed the slaughtered Lamb wherever he went, and they were not afraid to bear testimony. They were in fact faithful unto death.

So this great multitude, dressed in heavenly white, is a vision of the blessed dead. They are pictured at the end of their hard journey. They have marched out of tribulation and have joined the cherubim and seraphim, ceaselessly praising God beyond the reach of hunger or thirst or scorching heat. The Lamb will be their Shepherd forever, leading them to living water. Their prayer, "Deliver us from evil!" has not fallen on deaf ears but has received definitive answer. They have been rescued from every trial of life, and then, in two marvelous images, Revelation says that God will "shelter them" and will "wipe the tears from every eye" (7:15-17; 21:4).

The 144,000 and the Innumerable Host

Fundamentalists read these visions as confirmation of the view that God's attention will turn once more to the Jewish people after the faithful believers in Christ are caught up to God at the Rapture. After the Rapture of the church, the Four Horsemen will begin their terrible ride, but one result of the shower of coming calamities will be the conversion of 144,000 Jews (7:1-8). These Jews or Israelites will then take the Gospel to the Gentiles, and their work will be successful, since a countless host out of all nations will come to faith (7:9-17).

A liberationist reading sees in the 144,000 (7:1-8) a symbol of the church on earth, constituting by its faithfulness a powerful alternative community. The great unnumbered multitude in heaven (7:9-17) represents all who refuse to be integrated into the oppressive structures of the dominant culture. They are outside as well as inside the church, and so are not exactly coterminous with the 144,000. That they are unnumbered means that the triumph of these martyrs reaches beyond the limits of the organized church.

My own view is completely different from that of the fundamentalists and is very close to the liberationist reading. It seems to me that the Seer in Revelation 7 is offering us two separate and differing visions of the same fellowship of saints. Neither vision by itself can say all that needs to be said about God's people in the face of coming tribulation. John had two visions, and they complement one another. One helps explain the other, just as each succeeding vision throughout Revelation enriches and colors the mix of impressions left by earlier visions.

The opening scene of Revelation 7 (the 144,000) offers us a snapshot of one aspect of the life of God's people. They are meticulously numbered and they are sealed. The sealing and precise numbering indicate not only that they are God's own possession and enjoy God's personal protection. The sealing and numbering declare that they are God's army, holy warriors drawn up in their battle formations. The 144,000 are the whole community of the faithful in their earthly pilgrimage, sealed by God and protected, as they prepare to do battle against all anti-God powers.

The vast innumerable throng in the second half of the chapter (7:9-17) are the same faithful people portrayed at the beginning of the chapter. However, we now view them as standing before God at the end and goal of all their hard journeying. Their warfare is now ended.

Why the difference in the numbers? The precision of the 144,000 contrasts sharply with the vagueness of the idea that no one could number the multitude in the second vision. The first vision pictures the saints of God as they are sealed in preparation for the coming ordeal. The second vision is vague concerning the number, because it did not want to give the impression that every one who was sealed was automatically saved.

The Seer speaks of the 144,000 again in Rev 14:1-5. Features of the 144,000 (7:1-8) and of the innumerable throng (7:9-17) mingle and merge in that second description of the 144,000 (see also Dürer's woodcut number 13). There in Revelation 14, the Seer describes a multitude of 144,000, just as in Rev 7:1-8. They bear on their foreheads not the "seal" of God but "the name" of the Lamb and of God. Nevertheless the "seal" and the "name" mean the same thing: God's own possession, God's property! Like the second multitude of Rev 7 (7:9-17), the 144,000 in Revelation 14 stand before the throne of God, are led by the Lamb, and sing a song of salvation.

It seems as though Revelation could now go on to describe the breaking of the seventh seal and the glories of God's coming reign.

Chapter 9

Revelation 8:1-13

Seven Angels with Seven Trumpets

The blowing of the seven trumpets sets in motion catastrophes greater than those accompanying the snapping of the seven seals. Dürer shows us the opening events in this new series of seven. At the top of the woodcut seven angels at heaven's altar receive their trumpets directly from the hand of God, while an eighth angel throws fire down onto the earth (8:2-5).

The lower portion of Dürer's woodcut records the terrors which result from the blowing of the opening quartet of trumpets (8:6-12). Those first four angels bring destruction, just like the Four Horsemen (6:1-8).

Seven Angels
with Seven Trumpets
(Rev 8:1-13)

When the Lamb snaps open the seventh seal, an eerie silence descends on heaven for half an hour (8:1). Some liberationists think that silence in heaven means we should turn our attention to earth, that we should seek solutions not in the sky with God but on earth by human exertions. In fact, silence or passivity among people calling themselves Christians is one of the seven deadly sins in the catechism of liberationists. In that diagnosis they are surely correct, but what does the Seer himself hear in that heavenly silence?

For a moment the angels cease their unceasing hymns. The Lion does not roar, the Ox does not bellow, the Eagle stops shrieking, and the Human breaks off all speaking and shouting. The twenty-four elders let their hands drop away from playing their harps. The universe holds its breath. Anticipation mounts. Is this the calm before the final cosmic storm? What will the opening of the seventh seal bring? The end of the end? Not yet.

In the midst of solemn silence the Seer has a vision of the seven archangels who stand in the presence of God receiving seven trumpets from the hand of God (8:2). These angels are the same as the lamps before the throne of God (4:5; 5:6). Surely the seven angels with their seven trumpets will break the tension of the awful silence and usher in God's new world with a glorious fanfare (Joel 2:1; Matt 24:31; 1 Thess 4:16).

Dürer follows John in almost every detail. At the celestial altar, another angel, not one of the seven, holds the cover of a heavenly incense burner in the right hand. The prayers of the saints, mixed with incense, ascend like a little mushroom cloud to God (8:3-4). At the same time, the angel's left hand takes fire from the censer and throws it down onto the earth, filling the sky with thunder and lightning, and making the earth shake (8:5).

The meaning of this introductory scene is that God listens to the prayers of the saints and responds. Their prayers have been spelled out in Rev 6:10. There the saints cry out for the shortening of the time of tribulation and for the coming of God's reign. Their prayer is really not so different from the peti-tions of the Lord's Prayer. They pray for the coming of God's kingdom, for rescue from trial and tribulation, for full and final deliverance from evil.

This vision declares that God is not deaf to the prayers and pleadings of the saints. God's answer is to hand trumpets to the seven archangels. Will the trumpets usher in peace and joy? Yes, but not immediately. The blowing of the seven trumpets (8:2–11:19) will bring results even more terrible than the snapping of the seven seals (6:1–8:1).

The imagery of the trumpets is at one and the same time frightening and full of hope. The disasters or "plagues" (see 9:18-20) summoned up by the seven trumpets echo the plagues in Egypt in the days of the pharaoh oppressing Israel. Plagues seem like bad news instead of good. But those old plagues led step by terrible step to the liberation of the Hebrew slaves under Moses and Miriam at the time of the Exodus.

The seven trumpets in the hands of the seven archangels work even more powerfully than the blasts of the seven trumpets by which Joshua brought down the walls of ancient Jericho, as Israel entered the promised land (Josh 6:4-20). Trumpets punctuate the Scriptures. A terrible trumpet blast was heard at Sinai (Exod 19:16), and trumpets or shofars will herald the dawn of the Day of the Lord in the last times (Joel 2:1; Amos 3:6; Matt 24:31; 1 Cor 15:52; 1 Thess 4:16). At the end, trumpet blasts will signal the breakup of the entire old order of the cosmos, but that breaking up and breaking down is not to be dreaded as an exclusively negative act. God intends this destruction of the old to clear the way for the new creation.

The First Four Trumpets *(8:6-12)*

At the first trumpet blast, the Seer has a vision of hail and fire, mixed with drops of blood, raining down upon the earth, scorching a third of the trees and all the green grass (Rev 8:7; Exod 9:22-26; cf. Rev 16:8-9, 19-21). This is more severe than the harm worked by the Four Horsemen who were granted power over a fourth of the earth (6:8).

At the second trumpet blast, the Seer watches as something resembling a great mountain, burning with fire, "is thrown into the sea" (8:8). Dürer pictures a great volcano thrust down into the waters by a pair of powerful unearthly forearms. A third of the sea is turned to blood, so that a third of the sea creatures die, and a third of the world's ships are destroyed (8:9; Exod 7:20-21; Rev 16:3).

When the third trumpet sounds, a great burning star with the name "Wormwood" (Jer 9:15; 23:15; Lam 3:15) falls from heaven into the wells and springs of the earth, and a third of earth's waters become bitter, no longer fit for drinking (8:10-11). "Wormwood" is the name of a bitter herb known also in English as absinth and in Russian as *chernobyl*. Fundamentalists and other literalists saw the nuclear disaster of Chernobyl (1986) as a sign that the trumpets are blowing and we are living in the countdown days before the world's end. In his *Screwtape Letters* C. S. Lewis uses the name "Wormwood" for one of the junior devils. Dürer pictures the star Wormwood dropping into the square carved mouth of a well in the lower left.

A fourth angel trumpets, and the sun and moon and stars are stricken. A third of their light is kept from shining, thus dimming both day and night (8:12; Exod 10:21; Rev 6:12-13; 16:10). Dürer's sun and moon groan against a sky darkened by strong horizontal lines.

Three Woes *(8:13)*

The first four trumpets form a quartet, exactly like the Four Horsemen, and their work seems likewise destructive. After the initial four trumpet blasts, just as after the breaking of the first four seals and the galloping of the first four Riders, there is a break in the series of seven.

The fourth trumpet has sounded but for a moment the fifth angel hesitates. Into that brief interval of silence an eagle flies, soaring in midheaven. The eagle shrieks out a terrible message: "Woe, Woe, Woe!" That announcement means that four trumpet blasts may have sounded but three are still to come (8:13), and the final three will be more terrible than the opening quartet.

Faithful to the text of Revelation, Dürer pictures four angels blowing while three have yet to raise their trumpets to their lips. It is a crowded scene, and these angels are far less powerfully drawn than those in the preceding woodcut. They hardly look like the work of the same Artist.

Even more disturbing is the way one scene of doom follows another without relief. But again the message of the seven trumpets, woeful as they may be, is not merely negative. John's communities and our own should hear in the trumpets the distant triumph song and be heartened by the promise of a new genesis beyond the collapse of the old order.

And how shall we wait? Quietly and passively? Or actively and assertively? What can we do so that our lives begin to move right now in tune with the rhythms of those trumpets? How can we participate in God's critique of the old eon and in God's giving of the new creation? As in John's time, so in our own time, Christians differ in the answers they offer to these questions, but the questions refuse to go away, and they press us for our response.

Chapter 10

Revelation 9:1-21

The Fifth and Sixth Trumpets

In his eighth woodcut Dürer ignores the fifth trumpet (Rev 9:1-11). Instead he concentrates all his skill on rendering the events accompanying the blowing of the sixth trumpet. The sixth trumpet blast signals the release of four angels formerly bound at the Euphrates River. Those four angels, now unbound, bring terrible destruction upon the length and breadth of the earth (Rev 9:13-19).

It is in this context that Revelation first uses the word "plagues" as a description of the divinely ordained disasters falling upon the world (9:18-20). That word "plagues" offers an important clue. The disasters are meant, like the plagues in Egypt, to move hard hearts to repentance.

The Fifth and Sixth Trumpets
(Rev 9:1-21)

Dürer pictures God standing behind heaven's altar, distributing trumpets. God's brows are knit but is that a smile threatening to break out? Spikes of light radiate sharply from God's head. Four trumpets have blasted, and the final three trumpets, "the three woes" (8:13), must yet sound.

The Fifth Trumpet *(9:1-12)*

Dürer completely ignores the fifth trumpet which unleashes the first woe, probably because the monstrous locusts of the first woe (9:7-10) and the nightmarish riders of the second woe (9:17-19) look so much alike in John's vision. In this woodcut Dürer devotes his energies to portraying the riders of the second woe, which is identical with the sixth trumpet. As he does so, he follows the text of Revelation closely. But first a word about the part of the vision omitted by Dürer.

The Seer begins the series of three woes by telling how "a star" drops from heaven to earth. "Stars" in the ancient world were thought of as celestial beings, gods or demons or angels. A shooting star or especially a comet was a dreadful omen. The Seer tells how a fallen star wielding a great key opens the shaft of the bottomless pit or abyss (see Rev 11:7; Luke 8:31). Later the same angel (or is it another?) comes down to bind Satan and lock him into the pit for a thousand years (20:1).

When the "star" or fallen angel opens the bottomless pit, a cloud of black smoke belches forth out of the abyss, as out of some demonic blast-furnace, darkening the sun (9:1-2). And whirling out of the smoke comes a cloud of monstrous locusts. Dürer has included tiny locusts in his previous woodcut. They descend to earth in the flames of fire beneath the moon at the right hand side of his picture. They are an insignificant element in Dürer's woodcut, but in the Seer's Revelation they are terrible, otherworldly monsters. They look like horses ready for battle, with human faces and long hair like women and teeth like lions and the tails of scorpions. The beating of their wings sounds like horses and chariots rushing into battle (9:7-9; Prov 30:27).

They are dreadful, and yet for all their monstrosity, the power of this nightmarish horde to hurt people is strictly limited by God. They are not permitted to touch any people bearing the seal of God upon their foreheads (9:4), and they are set loose on the world only for "five months" (9:4-5), and they can injure but not kill (9:5).

This hellish army is under the command of a king or emperor called by the code name "Apollyon" or "Destroyer" (9:11). Apollyon is a pun on "Apollo," god of the sun and of rationality. Roman emperors were eager to identify themselves as incarnations of Apollo, and that may account for the Seer's choice of a name for this demonic king-leader. The Seer turns Roman propaganda upside down. According to the Seer, the emperor rules with dark powers from the abyss, not with the light of heaven!

The Sixth Trumpet *(9:13-19)*

Dürer passes over those monstrous locusts of the fifth trumpet (= first woe) and concentrates his artistry on the destructive force summoned up by the sixth trumpet announcing the second woe (9:13-21). Dürer pictures hard winds blowing from the four corners or horns of the golden altar of incense before God (8:3). Their counterparts, the four great angels, no longer held in check, throw themselves into their deadly work in earnest. The Four Winds and the Four Angels seem to be the same as the Four Horsemen of Revelation 6, simply viewed from a different angle. In fact, this woodcut (no. 8) of the Four Angels has much in common with the woodcut of the Four Horsemen (no. 4). The differing images portray the same dread powers, but now with their destructive force amplified.

As the Four Angels begin to swing their swords, "twice ten thousand times ten thousand" (= 200 million!) horses and riders pour across the Euphrates River (9:14-16; cf. 16:12-16). The Euphrates was one of the four fabled rivers of Eden (Gen 2:14). In historical times it was the boundary between Israel and its eastern enemy Babylon, and later it marked the border between the Roman Empire to the west and the dread Persian or Parthian empire to the east. The Seer envisions a fantastic throng of two hundred million warriors swarming across the borders into the Roman Empire, not merely to injure (cf. 9:5) but to kill. Dürer follows the text of Revelation closely, as he renders the Seer's vision of deadly invaders astride horses with lions' heads spouting fire and smoke and sulfur (= the three "plagues" of 9:18), while their tails sting like serpents (9:17). They came killing a third of humankind (9:15, 18).

Fundamentalists delight in noting that in 1965 Red China claimed to have a militia of two hundred million. They have used that claim in support of biblical literalism, anti-Communist sentiment, a strong U.S. military, and a sense that these are the last times.

Both Seer and Artist agree that no defense of rank or power is sufficient when the final judgment approaches. In Dürer's woodcut each destroying angel takes deadly aim on a different individual. In the lower right a pope with triple tiara lies among others wearing their insignia of ecclesiastical or secular power. In the lower left a soldier falls backwards off his horse.

His shining armor could not save him. Above him the third angel has seized a housewife by her hair and is poised to deliver a blow.

And then who is that bearded figure at the right margin staring horror-stricken at the fourth angel? Is it Dürer himself? Compare his face with the face of the bearded fellow sealed by the angel in the right foreground of woodcut number 6. Without exception, all must die. All, including the Artist himself, must one day give an account before the judgment seat of God.

The horrors or "woes" (9:12) associated with the Four Angels are explicitly called "plagues" (9:18, 20). That is John's reminder that, just as in the days when Moses struggled with Pharaoh in Egypt, so these final terrors at the end of times are not designed to drive people to despair. They are meant to provoke people to repentance before God. And yet, John laments, the six plagues were not successful in turning humankind from their idols of gold and silver and stone and wood. Nor did people cease their murders, sorceries, fornications, and thefts (9:20-21).

If these monstrous plagues failed in their purpose, what will God do next? Perhaps the seventh trumpet, announcing the third and final "woe," will be effective. We will see.

Chapter 11

Revelation 10:1–11

Another Mighty Angel

The sixth trumpet blast, freeing the four angels to work their terrible destructions, did not move humankind to repentance (9:20-21). What will come next? Revelation has brought us to the edge of the end, but again the end is delayed.

We expect the seventh trumpet, but John interrupts the series of trumpet visions to show us what he calls "another mighty angel." This angel has legs like pillars of fire and stands with one foot on dry land and the other in the sea. In one hand the angel holds a little open scroll. John is instructed to take the scroll and eat it. Then the angel swears with uplifted hand that there will be no more delay (John 10:1–11).

But delay there is. Before the blowing of the seventh trumpet, John is given a rod and told to measure the temple and its precincts except for the outer court (11:1-2). Measuring is a form of protection, as sealing is in Revelation 7. Immediately afterwards the same heavenly voice which instructed John to measure the temple recites to John a drama of two faithful witnesses (11:3-14).

When the seventh angel finally blows the seventh trumpet (11:15), we seem to be transported forward in time to the end of the world, as loud voices in heaven praise God for judging the nations and rewarding the saints (11:15-19). But even with the blowing of the seventh trumpet and its anticipation of the end, the end itself does not arrive. The Seer has yet more visions to share.

Dürer's ninth woodcut shows the great angel of Revelation 10, but Dürer omits all those other scenes that fill Revelation 11.

Another Mighty Angel
(Rev 10:1–11)

No More Delay (10:1-7)

A pause in the action interrupts the dramatic succession of trumpet blasts. Instead of the anticipated seventh trumpet and the hoped for climax of human history, the Seer reports a vision of a great angelic figure descending from heaven.

This figure, described as "another mighty angel" (10:1), resembles in many respects the exalted Christ of the first vision (Rev 1:9-20, woodcut 2). The Seer's report also echoes Daniel's older vision of his conversation with a mighty angel (Dan 10 and 12). That angel spoke to Daniel about the great trouble coming upon the world and about resurrection and judgment beyond. To Daniel was revealed "the book of truth" (Dan 10:21), but he was ordered to seal up the book until the time of the end (Dan 12:4).

Daniel asked, "How long must we wait?" The angel raised both hands to heaven and swore that the time would be short: a time (= one year) and times (= two years) and half a time (= six months; see Dan 12:6). That prophesied time is the same as forty-two months (Rev 11:2) or three and a half years (Rev 11:9) or 1,260 days (Rev 12:6).

John's vision connects with Daniel's more ancient vision and implies that the time of trouble announced to Daniel has now finally arrived. Deliverance lies on the far side of the final, prophesied trouble.

John sees the mighty angel descending from heaven, wrapped in a cloud like a white robe (cf. 1:13). A rainbow arches over his head, and his face shines like the sun (1:14). His two legs are not burnished bronze (1:16) but are like columns of fire. Stars often mean angels in Revelation (see 1:20), and a star-angel with two legs is a vision inspired by a comet with two tails.

Daniel saw two angels, one standing on each side of the Tigris River (Dan 12:5). John sees a single mighty angel plant one fiery foot on the sea and the other on the land, signaling the all-encompassing significance of his authoritative message.

The angel holds a little scroll, and it is not sealed (5:1) but open. Holding the scroll, the angel shouts, and his voice echoes and reechoes, like a lion roaring, like seven thunders pealing (10:1-4).

John's immediate reaction is to begin writing down what he hears in that thunder, but the angel sharply commands him not to write but instead to "seal up" the message (10:4). Strange! This is the opposite of the unsealing in chapters 5 and 6. Does this odd command mean that the end will not arrive as speedily as anticipated? That for a short time the will of God must remain unfulfilled and the face of God must stay hidden from the vast company of humankind? More likely this strange passage indicates that, beyond the rumblings of thunder and roaring as of a lion (10:3-4), is a clear word of God, as open and plain as writing in a book (10:8), for those who have ears to hear it. And this word of God is good news for all God's people (10:7).

With right hand uplifted to heaven, the angel swears a solemn oath that there will be "no further delay" (v. 6) in the fulfilling of the mysterious plan of God. At the sounding of the seventh trumpet, the "mystery of God," the plan of God hidden for ages in prophecy and promise, will become a reality on earth (10:5-7).

Eat the Scroll (10:8-11)

Then the Seer hears a voice commanding him to take the open scroll from the hand of the mighty angel (10:8). So John asks for the scroll, and the angel gives it to him with the command, "Take it and eat" (10:9). The winged angel at the top of Dürer's woodcut represents the heavenly voice directing him to go to the angel and take the scroll.

In John's mouth the scroll is as sweet as honey, but in his stomach it tastes bitter (10:9-10; Ezek 2:8–3:3). The message is not the Seer's own. God gave it to him. It may even be distasteful to him. Certainly it is unpleasant and difficult. And yet he must swallow it, ingest it, let it soak into his bones.

This little scroll, given to the Seer to eat, is apparently the same scroll described in chapter 5, the one whose seventh seal was broken in 8:1. The scroll is open, and John has the bittersweet task of continuing to prophesy about many peoples and nations and tongues and kings (cf. 10:11).

Dürer pictures John's unfinished book lying open at his side. His pen and ink are ready. He has written what he has seen so far (Rev 1–9), and he is being called now in a second commissioning to complete the task which he has begun. Up to this point readers have patiently endured visions that often seem about as clear as claps of thunder or the roaring of a lion. Now they are promised clarity, if only they will continue reading the Seer's words a little longer.

Measuring the Temple *(11:1-3)*

Dürer found no room in his woodcut for the remaining events of this interlude between the sixth and seventh trumpets. The Artist has omitted almost everything in Revelation 11, but we should at least scan the contents of this amazing chapter.

At the beginning of chapter 11 the Seer is given a measuring rod and told to "measure the temple of God and the altar and the people worshiping there." At the same time he is instructed not to measure "the court outside the temple" but to exclude it, because it is "given over to the nations" who will trample the holy city for forty-two months (11:1-2; see on 12:6).

What's going on here? In one of his earliest letters Paul spoke of the Christian community as "the temple" of God (1 Cor 3:16). Here John also uses temple language (cf. Rev 3:12) but he wants to distinguish two groups of Christians in the community. By "the temple and the altar and the people worshiping there" he means faithful insiders. But then who does John mean by "the outer court"? Apparently he has in mind weak and vacillating members of the community.

To all that John adds the image of "measuring." Measuring means protection (as in Zech 2:1-5). In the earlier interlude, between the breaking of the sixth and seventh seals, the faithful were sealed and numbered (Rev 7), also images of protection.

The command to measure the worshipers at the altar indicates that the core members, the innermost circle, the genuinely faithful worshipers of God will be protected. The "outer court" is John's name for members of the community lacking the spirit of loyalty and patience. They will not be measured and so may lose faith during the coming time of testing. This is a summons to Christians to self-examination. Are they truly faithful, or are they lukewarm (3:16), lacking the required commitment?

The Two Witnesses *(11:4-14)*

Dürer has also omitted from his woodcut the martyrdom and subsequent resurrection of the "two witnesses" described by John in the middle section of the chapter (11:4-13).

It is not easy to pin down the identity of these two witnesses with precision and confidence. Readers have seen in them echoes of various pairs of significant personages in biblical story. In much early and medieval Christian thinking as well as in some Reformation interpretation, the two witnesses were identified as Enoch and Elijah. Many today think that the Seer is conjuring up the images of Moses and Elijah, those great ancient witnesses to the truth of God, who appeared in holy connection with Jesus on the Mount of Transfiguration (Mark 9:2-13). The two witnesses have the power of Moses to turn water to blood (11:6; cf. Exod 7:14-25) and like Elijah they can shut up the heavens so that no rain falls (11:6; cf. 1 Kgs 17:1; 18:1).

Or should we think of John the Baptist and Jesus, the forerunner and the Messiah, both of whom suffered martyrdom? Or Peter and Paul, those great foundational figures of the church's first generation? Both were martyred, and so both were dishonored on earth but affirmed and glorified by God.

Whoever sat for the portrait of these two witnesses, the imagery leaves no doubt about the fact that they stand for the church in its vocation and destiny. The Seer calls these two witnesses "the two olive trees and the two lampstands that stand before the Lord of the earth" (11:4). These phrases echo the language of the prophet Zechariah who so referred to Joshua the priest and Zerubbabel, the governor. Those two were anointed by God to lead Israel in the hard days after the Babylonian exile (Zech 4:3, 14).

If he is alluding to priest and governor, the Seer is once again identifying the community of believers as having both political and priestly character. They are "a kingdom and priests" (1:6; 5:10; 20:6), a community of people organized under the sovereignty of God to resist the dominant political culture and to render priestly service to God alone. As "olive trees" and "lampstands" they are called to be brightly burning oil lamps, bearing witness in an alien culture to the truth of God. That is the church's calling, and it is neither easy nor safe.

It is in this context that for the first time in Revelation we meet "the Beast" who plays such a prominent role beginning in chapter 13. Having come up out of the bottomless pit (see 9:1-3), the Beast directs all its ugly power against the two witnesses, killing them

(11:7). The faithfully witnessing church will provoke deadly opposition.

The corpses of the two witnesses lie untended and unburied in the streets of the city which is called allegorically "Sodom and Egypt" (11:8). And the Seer says that Jesus was crucified in that city. John seems to be saying that any city or nation which oppresses the saints is as vile as Sodom, as cruel as Egypt, and as callous as Jerusalem. All three were places of idolatry, injustice, and contempt for God.

For a very brief time ("three and a half days," see 12:6 and 13:5) their enemies gaze on their unburied bodies and even celebrate the death and humiliation of the two witnesses (11:9-10). But then the witnesses are resurrected, and a loud voice publicly summons them to "Come up here" to God in heaven (11:11-12). And their resurrection and ascension are accompanied by an earthquake, decimating the oppressor city. "Two" is the number of the faithful witnesses, but "seven times a thousand" is the number of oppressors killed at their resurrection. Many finally begin to give God glory (11:13).

Whether we think the "two witnesses" are foreshadowed in Moses and Elijah or in Joshua and Zerubbabel or in some other faithful pair, the bottom line is that the Seer is struggling to find language to stiffen the backbone of the hardpressed members of the Seven Churches. The entire store of the Seer's rich imagery aims to encourage his hearers to defy the Beast and be faithful witnesses to God's subversive truth. That truth, the Seer says, is a "torment" to the earthbound (11:10).

The Seer is convinced that the faithful will meet terrible opposition as they witness to God. The Beast will make war on them and for a time will conquer and kill them. They will not be raptured before the trouble, as most fundamentalists think, but they will be strengthened and accompanied by God as they walk through the dark valley. And in the end the witnessing community will triumph. The forces of the Beast are led by one called "the Destroyer" (9:11; cf. 11:18), but God is a God of life, whose word calls into being that which is not, whose breath enlivens the dead (11:12), whose power of creation is not limited by the Beast's power to destroy.

The Seventh Trumpet *(11:15-19)*

Finally, after the digression reporting the vision of the mighty angel with the little scroll (10:1-11), after the command to measure the temple (11:1-3), and after report about the fate of the two witnesses (11:4-14), the seventh angel blows the seventh trumpet (11:15). At the blaring of that trumpet, loud voices in heaven celebrate the end and goal of history in an astonishing phrase: "The kingdom of the world has become the kingdom of our Lord and of his Christ" (11:15).

The Bible regularly and deliberately uses political language in giving voice to the deepest spiritual longings. Jesus himself announced his own program in the cry, "The kingdom of God has drawn near" (Mark 1:15; see on Rev 1:9). The Apocalypse speaks more negatively than any other New Testament writing about "the kingdoms of this world." It sharply opposes earthly rule as evil versus God's rule as alone good. The Seer would probably have found it impossible to say with Paul that "the governing authorities have been ordained by God" (Rom 13:1). And how could he honor the emperor or pray for the emperor, as other New Testament writers asked? (1 Pet 2:13; 1 Tim 2:1-2).

In the eye of the Seer, the Roman Empire was idolatrous and blasphemous through and through. In its propaganda Rome exalted itself as the world's light and salvation, and it called on the peoples of earth to adore Rome for her benefits. The Seer clearly perceived how easily humankind falls into the sin of absolutizing powerful benefactors. He sees a time coming when all systems of domination and idolatry will be overthrown. Their destruction is the third "woe" (8:13; 11:14). The good news beyond all woes is that the kingdoms of this world will be replaced by God's own good governance.

For the third time in Revelation (see 4:9 and 7:12), the twenty-four elders break forth into a hymn of thanksgiving. Here in this third song they praise God whose "wrath" (see notes on 6:12-17) makes the raging of the nations cease and destroys the destroyers of the earth (11:16-18).

Dürer uses pictures, not words, but still manages to portray heaven's celebration. He skips the twenty-four elders and the flashes of lightning and the heavy hail (11:19), but he shows cherubs and a rainbow surrounding the ark of the covenant, sign of God's mercy and justice (11:19).

In spite of the song of celebration (11:15-18), the book of Revelation does not end with the blowing of the seventh trumpet. The Seer has yet more to say about the tribulations before describing the triumph of God's people. Yet this hymn announces ahead of time that the tribulations and struggle about to be described in chapters 12–19 will result in total victory for God and the people of God.

10:1–11:19 as Synopsis

The varied scenes of this interlude (10:1–11:19) can be as puzzling as they are revealing. It has helped me to think of these scenes as a kind of book of Revelation in miniature: the Seer is called by a great heavenly figure to a prophetic vocation and is given insight into God's plan inscribed on a scroll (Rev 1–5; 10:1-11). He is told that some of God's people will enjoy divine protection while others will apparently stumble in the coming trials (Rev 6–7; 11:1-3). The church as a whole is a community of witnesses to the truth of God (11:4-6) and should bear witness even though the Beast will wage war on the church, producing many martyrs (11:7-10). In heaven's good time God will raise up the martyr church and defeat the Beast (11:11-13). The series ends, as the whole of Revelation ends, with rapturous praise of God's victory and rejoicing in the coming of God's uncontested sovereignty (11:15-19).

So this series of scenes (10:1–11:19) offers a kind of synopsis of the entire Apocalypse. By replaying the plot and rehearsing basic themes, these two chapters help to keep us readers oriented to the flow and direction of the book as a whole.

Dolphin or Dragon?

Behind the mighty angel in his woodcut Dürer has drawn a scene that appears astonishingly tranquil and ordinary after all the terrors of the first six trumpets. Swans glide peacefully, and boaters lounge on the water with merchant vessels sailing off in the distance. Is that Dürer's way of celebrating the advent of God's sovereignty announced by the blowing of the seventh trumpet?

And what is that off to the left of the woodcut? A friendly dolphin playing in the waters near Patmos? Or is it the ugly snout of a horned monster rising up from the depths of the sea (11:7)?

Chapter 12

Revelation 12:1-6, 13-17

The Woman and the Dragon

John sees two omens or signs in the sky. The first is a Heavenly Woman, clothed with the sun, standing on the crescent of the moon, crowned with twelve stars, and she is pregnant with her firstborn. The second is the Great Red Dragon, identified by John as the Devil or Satan, the primordial Serpent, the deceiver of humankind (12:9).

With an arrogant sweep of its tail, the Dragon pulls down a third of heaven's stars (12:4) and gets ready to devour the Woman's Child, as soon as it is born (12:4-5). But the Child escapes, snatched up to God's throne in heaven (12:5).

The Woman flees on eagles' wings to refuge in the wilderness (12:13-14). The Dragon pursues the Woman and pours out from its mouth a river of water to engulf and drown her (12:15). But the earth defends the Woman, opening its mouth and swallowing the river (12:16). In anger the Dragon stalks off, determined to make war on the rest of the Woman's offspring (12:17).

In Dürer's woodcut, one of the Dragon's heads, spewing forth the river, casts a menacing look in our direction. The Dragon is not yet defeated.

The Woman and the Dragon
(Rev 12:1-6, 13-17)

When the seventh trumpet blasted (11:15), heaven burst forth with anthems of rejoicing at God's victory (11:15-18), and yet the end is once more delayed. John sees first one and then a second "portent" or sign in the heavens. First John sees a woman whose clothing is the sun. Her feet rest on a crescent moon, and she wears on her head a royal diadem of 12 stars (12:1).

A Woman of Light and the Great Red Dragon *(12:1-6)*

Dürer's picture is so composed that an invisible diagonal line crosses the woodcut from upper right to lower left, yielding two triangles. The upper-left triangle contains the heavenly and the holy, while the lower-right triangle is dominated by the demonic and the ugly.

Dürer has filled the heavenly triangle with emblems of light. Just as in the Seer's vision, a crescent moon glows beneath the Woman's feet, and twelve stars form a gleaming diadem for her head (12:1). A whole multitude of stars spangle the sky in the two upper corners of Dürer's woodcut. Beams of light stream from the Woman and from God. Dürer has left white open spaces in his heavenly section, giving the impression of luminosity and brightness and light. Dürer's Woman, bursting with inner light, is a picture of perfect joy and tranquillity. The Seer, however, describes her as pregnant and crying out in the agony of labor pains (12:2).

The lower earthy triangle is dark. Crisscrossed with lines, it is almost fully occupied by the second portent appearing in the heavens: the Great Red Dragon. Here Dürer faithfully follows the Seer's script. Both Seer and Artist picture a powerful Dragon with seven heads and ten horns, and a diadem tops each of its heads (12:3). In an earlier biblical apocalypse, Daniel had a vision of four monstrous beasts, and among them those four had a total of seven heads and ten horns (Dan 7). The Seer never quotes Daniel but he seems to be under the spell of that earlier visionary.

Dürer's Dragon is an ugly monster, stepping up onto the earth out of a pit of darkness, like some slimy creature crawling out from under a rock. The Dragon is a composite of real and fabled beasts. In addition to horns, it has fangs and claws, feathers and scales, legs and wings, ugly heads carried on serpentine necks, and it is arrogant. With its great tail it attacks heaven, sweeping a third of the stars down out of God's sky (12:4). The Dragon not only sweeps them down but sweeps them up into his own dark legions. We have seen earlier that "stars" may mean "angels" (1:20; 9:1). What the Seer reports is described elsewhere as the Devil's revolt against God. In fact in the very next section (12:7-12) the Seer will describe war in heaven, as the Dragon with "his angels" makes war on Michael and his host of good angels.

In the Seer's text and in Dürer's woodcut we are witnessing the dread onslaught of the darkness upon the light. Ancient people were fascinated by the way night swallows up day, once every twenty-four hours, and how day is reborn every morning as the sun mounts up high and strong. The ancients contemplated the strong annual return of the powers of night beginning at midsummer, commencing the annual decline of the sun towards the winter solstice and the sun's resurgence. Myths spoke of the warfare between light and dark in terms of unrelenting struggle between order and chaos, good and evil.

Seer and Artist alike declare that the primeval conflict between light and darkness, between day and night, is being reenacted in the contest between the Woman and the Dragon. Roman emperors portrayed themselves on their coins as the incarnations of Apollo the Sun-God, as champions of light, as bringers of civilizing order to an otherwise chaotic Mediterranean world. The Seer, however, understands the empire as being the tool of the Dragon, the aggressive enemy of light, in league with the prince of darkness.

The terrible struggle between good and evil, light and darkness, marks human history as a whole. It is too easy, too superficial, to think in terms of a warfare between a good church and an evil empire. In the seven letters (Rev 2–3) the Seer reminds us in the most emphatic terms that light and dark struggle to gain the upper hand inside every human community, including the church.

Both the Seer and the Artist picture the Dragon as standing full of menace before the Woman. This is a vision of terror. It is not just Dragon versus Woman, but mighty Dragon with seven heads and seven royal diadems and ten horns threatening a pregnant woman in her hour of greatest vulnerability. The evil intent of the Dragon is clear. The instant her child is born, the Dragon plans to devour it (12:4).

In God's good time the Woman bears her son (12:5), who fulfills the hope of Psalm 2 for a Messiah who will conquer the arrogant nations with a rod of iron and rule over them.

The Dragon lunges to devour the child, but God enters the picture and thwarts the Dragon's plan by catching the child up to heaven (12:5).

In all the busyness of Dürer's woodcut, the Woman's newborn child, lofted heavenward by a pair of cherubs, is in danger of being lost from our view. The child is so small, and our eye begins to wander from one detail to another.

And yet the artist takes pains to focus our attention. First, he places the child in the center of the upper triangle. Then the Woman assumes an attitude of prayer and directs her own gaze and ours toward the child. God, half hidden by a surround of clouds, looks downward and gently raises a hand of blessing toward the approaching child. In the far upper-left corner of Dürer's woodcut, an angel (not to be found in the text of Revelation) points to the child with every element of his angelic form: with eyes, clasped hands, knees, and most of all with the long slender feathers of that great left wing.

Defeated in its desire to eat the child, the Dragon turns on the Woman. When her child is taken up to God, the Woman flies on eagle's wings into the wilderness, often a sanctuary for God's people (12:6, 14; Ps 78:52).

There in her wilderness-refuge, says the Seer, she is nourished by God for 1,260 days. 1,260 days (11:3; 12:6) is the same as forty-two months (11:2; 13:5) or "a time (one year) and times (two years) and half a time (six months)" (6:14), and signifies a period of distress limited by God's own providence and power.

The number has its source in the book of Daniel (7:25; 12:7).

The Wrath of the Dragon *(12:13-18)*

Both Seer and Artist picture the enormously agitated Dragon pouring from its foul mouth a whole river of water in a fierce attempt to drown the Woman (12:15). But again God intervenes. At God's command, the earth opens its mouth and swallows up that river, frustrating the Dragon's evil intent (12:16). In a fit of rage, the Dragon stomps off, determined to make war on "the rest of her children" (12:17). Who are they? And who exactly is this Woman?

The Woman of Revelation 12

At one level the Woman is Mary, the mother of Jesus. Her child is the long-awaited Christ. Stalked by Satan his whole life long, he seemed to be devoured, swallowed up at the Cross. But his obedient and trusting march to the Cross was paradoxically his triumph. He was caught up to heaven in his death and resurrection. But this Woman is more than any individual woman, even Mary. In Revelation, the number 12 with its multiples seems always to refer to God's people, and this heavenly Woman wears twelve stars as her crowning glory. She personifies Heavenly Light, and with her starry crown symbolizes the conviction that the faithful are children of light, persecuted by the prince of darkness.

So this heavenly Woman of John's vision is the whole people of God throughout all the eons of history, both Israel and the new community down to the present time. "The rest of her children" are all the people of God in their earthly pilgrimage, described by the Seer as those who obey God and hold onto the testimony of Jesus (Rev 12:17).

Both the Seer with his words and the Artist with his woodcut offer us a victory scene. At the midpoint of Revelation, after the terrors of the seven seals and the seven trumpets, the Seer is granted a vision of ultimate triumph. In Jesus' life and death and resurrection God has won a great victory. At the same time we are introduced to "the great red dragon" who has been cast down out of heaven (cf. Luke 10:8) and is frustrated in his attack on the light. Fallen from heaven and frustrated, but not destroyed. Not yet.

Chapter 13

Revelation 12:7-12

War in Heaven

John is witness to a colossal War in Heaven. Michael with his angels joins battle with the Dragon and his angels. Defeated by Michael and his hosts, the Dragon is cast from heaven down onto the earth. A loud voice in heaven celebrates, "Rejoice, you heavens! But woe to you, earth and sea, because the devil has come down to you full of anger!" (12:7-12). Brimming with wrath, the Dragon goes off to make war on the Woman's children, the Christian community (12:17).

Dürer has captured the terrible energy of the heavenly combat between the hosts of Michael and those of the Dragon in one of his most powerful woodcuts.

War in Heaven

(Rev 12:7-12)

Seer and Artist describe a great "war in heaven" with Michael and his angels fighting the Dragon and his angels (12:7). Meanwhile, beneath the glowering sky where the battle rages fiercely, Dürer's earth is all peace and prosperity. How can this be? Isn't earth tormented, blasted, nearly destroyed by this time? The earlier chapters of Revelation are filled with scenes of slaughter, with earthquake and eerie eclipse, with stars falling from the sky, with convulsions on the sea and terrible invasions from the east. The seven seals have been broken, and the seven trumpets have blared. The result has been terror on all sides.

Once again it is important not to read the visions of Revelation as occurring one after the other in neat chronological order. Revelation is full of anticipations and flashbacks. And some visions are repetitions of others in slightly altered form and so are commentaries on them.

Revelation 12 unmasks the historical struggles of the faithful and shows that they are not fighting against flesh and blood alone, not against "Jezebel" and "Balaam" alone, not even against the emperor and his economic and religious policies alone. They are involved in a struggle of cosmic dimensions, the warfare between darkness and light, the Dragon and the Woman, the Dragon with his angels and Michael with his, the ancient warfare between Satan and God.

In Revelation 12, the Seer skillfully wraps his report of the war in heaven (12:7-12) within the two parts of his message about the Woman and the Dragon (12:1-6 and 13-17), inviting us to contemplate these varied visions as a complex unity. In Dürer's woodcut the archangel Michael, while leaning hard on his spear, glances to his right (our left). His eyes nudge us to look in the same direction, back to the preceding scene, so that we connect these two woodcuts as alternative portraits of the same spiritual struggle.

The Seer declares that "war broke out in heaven," with Michael and his angels entering into mortal combat against the Dragon and his angels (12:7). The Seer doubtless envisioned myriads of the hosts of heaven allied to Michael warring against countless thousands of rebellious angels. The angels were thought to be as numerous as the stars in the sky. The stars, sparkling mysteriously in the heavens, were considered to be angels by many ancient people (see Rev 1:20; 9:1; 12:4). The Artist once again draws not a whole army of angels but four awesome figures (as in woodcuts 6 and 8). Four great angels fill the upper portion of the woodcut with their powerfully sculpted bodies, full of light and energy. The ferocity of the warfare and its great cost are expressed in the horizontal black lines of the terrible dark sky.

The archangel Michael heaves with all his angelic weight on a long barbed spear, impaling the Dragon, laboring mightily to force the Dragon down out of the sky. The archangel frowns and seems almost to break out in sweat with the enormous exertion.

A second angel takes careful aim with bow and arrow on one of the Dragon's dread army. Two other angels are poised to cut and strike with their sharp swords. The wings and shields of all four angels form a solid and impenetrable barrier, not only blocking the demons from heaven, but pressing them backwards, throwing them down to earth.

Michael and the Dragon

The Dragon is defined here as "the ancient serpent" also known as "the Devil and Satan." Having deceived Adam and Eve near creation's dawning, the Dragon continues the business of deceiving up to the present time and can be named quite simply as "the deceiver of the whole world" (12:9).

In biblical tradition Michael is the guardian angel of Israel (Dan 12:1). In the context of Revelation 12 Michael is a Christ figure. He has struggled in a decisive battle and has gained the upper hand. A great battle has been won in the sky, but the war continues in a new arena. Just so, the New Testament pictures Jesus as "binding" Satan (Mark 3:27), "triumphing" over him (Col 2:15), or "casting him down" (Luke

10:18; John 12:31). In Michael as Christ figure or in Jesus himself, God has won a great victory. Nevertheless, history did not end with Christ's death and resurrection. Far from it. The Devil still prowls the earth, even more furiously than before, seeking to snatch and devour. The full and final victory of light lies in the future.

Woe to the Earth

John's universe seems to be three-storied: heaven above, earth in the center, and the dreary underworld far below. A great victory has been won in heaven. Satan has been cast out, so that heaven is now a Satan-free zone. But the Dragon has come down to earth where the struggle not only continues but now even intensifies. Therefore a loud voice in heaven cries out, "Woe to you, earth and the sea!" (12:12).

Later the devil will be swept off the earth and confined in the underworld (20:1-3). Finally, after one last ineffective assault, the devil will be cast into the lake of fire (20:10). Then the entire universe—the heavens and the earth and the underworld—will be completely free of Satan. Then and only then will there be a genuinely new heaven and a new earth (21:1).

Dürer pictures the clash of angels and demons. It is a moment of horrific violence in the heavens. But look again at the earth below, all calm and quiet. That is Dürer's way of saying that the earth is often uncomprehending and ignorant of the spiritual warfare. Seer and Artist agree that earth and its inhabitants are too often simply unaware of the heights and depths of the struggle for the soul of humankind. Revelation and other passages of the New Testament sometimes describe the coming of the end as the climax of a series of disasters that should have been read as clear warning signals (Mark 13:1-31). But elsewhere, sometimes in the same context, the end is described as coming like a thief in the night, when disasters are absent, when people everywhere are saying, "Peace, peace" (1 Thess 5:3; Mark 13:32-37). These variations reveal the folly of trying to "read the signs" in terms of calculating the precise moment when the end will occur. But most of all they signal how easy it is for the faithful to lapse into spiritual lethargy and laziness.

God alone knows the hour, the day and the year (Mark 13:33). John's visions should not be treated like so many bits and pieces of a calendar crying out for readers to manipulate them and order them into a reliable timetable. The visions are not a puzzle to be solved. They are a divine summons to constant wakefulness, a call to enter the struggle against evil and injustice, and a vivid promise of eventual victory.

Meanwhile, filled with wrath at being banished from heaven and cast down onto the earth, the Dragon goes off to make war on the Woman's offspring, the people of the new community (12:17). His attack will be ferocious, because the Dragon knows his days are numbered. His strategy is wickedly ingenious, as we shall see.

Chapter 14

Revelation 13:1-18

The Beast Whose Number Is 666

Cast out of heaven, the Dragon (identified as the devil or Satan, the ancient Serpent) summons two beasts, one from the sea, one from the land, to act as his earthly agents in his warfare on God's people. The first beast, with seven heads and ten horns, has the power of the Dragon, and its number, we are told, is 666. The second beast, with two horns like the Lamb, compels people to receive the mark of the beast.

The twelfth of Dürer's woodcuts shows people of the earth adoring the beast. The worshipers of the beast in this woodcut, as in Dürer's first woodcut, are of every rank and class, and all of them look quite respectable!

Dürer pictures God enthroned in heaven and adored by angels far above earth's adoration of the beasts. God and one of a trio of angels hold sickles. They are ready for the "harvest" of judgment day! Another angel, hefting a large wooden cross, is poised to strike at the beast with a sword. In fact the cross is God's secret weapon.

The Beast Whose Number Is 666
(Rev 13:1-18)

Defeated in the sky, ejected from heaven, the Dragon takes his stand on the shore of the sea (12:18) and calls up two beasts who with the Dragon form an evil trinity (13:1, 11). The two monstrous agents of Satan dominate the lower half of Dürer's woodcut.

The First Beast *(13:1-10)*

The Beast from the sea in the lower right looks almost exactly like the Dragon (woodcut 10). Just as the Christ is the very image and incarnation of God, so the Beast is the incarnation of evil. Like the Dragon, the first Beast has seven heads and ten horns. Where the Dragon has seven diadems, the first Beast has ten (13:1). What that means is that the fullness of the power of the Dragon ("seven") is parceled out among ten earthly rulers. Those ten rulers are either a succession of ten Roman emperors, or they are ten puppet kings allied to the Romans. Either way, in John's view the Roman Empire as a massive system of political and economic power was the instrument of Satan and posed a severe threat to the existence of the church as a community of faith.

In portraying the beasts, the Seer once more makes use of an old biblical tradition without directly quoting it. The prophet Daniel (Dan 7) envisioned four successive empires in the form of four beasts ripping and tearing at the people of God: a Lion (Babylon), a Bear (the Medes), a Leopard (Persia), and a fourth dreadful Beast with iron teeth and ten horns (the Empire of Alexander of Macedon and his successors). By John's day the fourth and final beast of Daniel's vision was no longer interpreted as the Greek Empire of Alexander but was identified with the Roman Empire, since Rome had become the dominant world power, ruling from the border of Persia in the east all the way to the straits of Gibraltar in the west.

In the Seer's vision various features of the Danielic beasts are mixed and mingled. So the first Beast of Revelation is part leopard, part bear, and part lion. It has previously been described as coming up from the "abyss" or "bottomless pit," the bleak arena of death

and of Satan's authority (9:1; 11:7). Here the Beast is said to emerge "from the sea" (13:1). That description connects the first Beast with the great sea monster Leviathan. Egypt's feared hippopotamus and crocodile were the prototypes for the mythic monsters Behemoth and Leviathan (Job 40–41). They were symbols of the chaos always threatening God's ordered creation.

In his description of the two beasts summoned up by the Dragon, John taps into the fear of those nightmarish creatures thrashing about deep in the psyche of Israel. At the same time, by describing the advent of the first Beast as "from the sea," John tips us off that he is applying these ancient images to the Roman governor of the province of Asia. The governor arrived annually by boat from Rome, greeted by some in Asia as an emissary of light, but John sees him emerging from the sea like the primeval chaos monster.

The Seer draws our attention to how one of the heads of the first Beast has been struck a fatal blow, and yet the awful wound has healed, astonishing the whole world (13:3). That blow to one head is often interpreted on the background of the death of the Roman emperor Nero. When Nero committed suicide in the year 68, the Roman Empire was plunged into civil war as a series of claimants struggled to gain the upper hand over one another. The empire teetered for a short time on the brink of chaos but then quickly recovered its central power. So the Roman beast was mortally wounded but was then shortly "resurrected."

John carefully spells out parallels between the wounded and recovering empire on the one hand, and the mortally wounded and resurrected Christ on the other. The devil always imitates God in the evil effort to look like God and so lead humanity astray.

In his woodcut Dürer ignores the wounding and recovery of the empire. He seems fascinated instead with another aspect of the Beast: its blasphemous mouth. The coins of ancient Rome, handled in common daily transactions, gave the emperors titles that really belong to God, calling the emperor "Lord" and "divine" and naming the emperors as source of "salvation," "liberty," and "peace."

As the Dragon with its tail arrogantly swept a third of the stars down out of God's sky (12:4) and waged war on the angels of heaven (12:7-12), so the Beast blasphemes God and God's name, and it battles against God's people (13:5-6). The Dragon in its wrath plotted war on the Woman's offspring (12:17), and as the Dragon's agent, the first Beast made war on the saints (13:7).

With its astonishing power the Beast was successful in gaining authority over people of every tribe and tongue and nation (13:7). All the "inhabitants of the earth" (13:8) worshiped the Beast. Who exactly are these "inhabitants of the earth"? Is that a code word for the earth-bound? For the heaven-deniers? These worshipers of the Beast are very clearly defined as all whose names are not inscribed in the book of the slain but living Lamb (13:8).

Life and death gain fresh definitions here, as the Seer writes of "the Book of Life of the slaughtered Lamb" or "murdered Lamb" (13:8). "Life" and "slaughter" or "murder" would seem to be opposites! And yet they form a fresh and startling combination in the career of the Lamb. Godly life springs forth from the cross and grave, and ironically all who follow the Lamb will live even though they die.

After his astonishing redefinition of life and death, the Seer quotes the prophet Jeremiah and summons the churches once more to endurance and faith. They may suffer captivity or sword (13:10), but they must remember that their names are indelibly inscribed in "the Book of Life" which belongs to the Lamb who was slain (13:8).

The Second Beast *(13:11-18)*

Then the Seer beholds a second Beast. It rises not from the sea like the first Beast, but "out of the earth" (13:11). In ancient Hebrew mythology the terrible chaos monster Behemoth was paired with the sea monster Leviathan (see 13:1). Here in the context of Revelation, the fact that the second Beast rises from the earth indicates that in contrast to the first Beast, an import from across the waters, this second Beast is a native institution.

The first Beast, like Leviathan, comes from the sea and means the Roman governor, the incarnation of Roman imperial might in the province of Asia. The second Beast, like Behemoth, is at home on the land. It symbolizes the native Asian priesthood of the seven cities presiding enthusiastically over the cult of impe-

rial Rome, beating the drum for the worship of Roma (Rome personified as a goddess) and of the emperor (honored as a deity in Asia Minor).

The second Beast has two horns like a lamb, but its voice is the voice of the Dragon (13:11). Dürer draws a lion with a ram's horns. Later the Seer calls this second Beast "the false prophet" (Rev 16:13; 19:20; 20:10). Its function is to mimic the work of the Holy Spirit and all true prophecy. It makes propaganda for the first Beast. It gives breath to the image of the first Beast (13:15), in a parody of the Holy Spirit's life-breathing work. With words and wonders it deceives the inhabitants of the earth, leading them to worship the image of the first Beast while persecuting all who refuse (13:12-15).

How can anyone possibly resist the Dragon and the Beasts? Aren't their powers in fact irresistible? What would happen to anyone who dared to defy them and to worship God alone?

The Number of the Beast Is 666 *(13:16-18)*

John's vision concludes with the notorious reference to the "mark of the beast" and the number 666. The second Beast does its evil worst to compel all people to be marked on the right hand or the forehead with the mark of the first Beast (13:16). Just as the 144,000 were sealed with God's name (7:2; 14:1), so those who are not God's own are also stamped or sealed, but with the name of the Beast.

Without the mark, people can neither buy nor sell (13:17). Refusal to bear the mark of the Beast may mean that some Christians shunned the use of common Roman coins, which bore the image and name or "mark" of the emperor (see Mark 12:13-17). If conscientious Christians like John refused to use the offensive coins, they cut themselves off from participation in the economic life of their cities and so barred themselves from sharing in the prosperity of their cities. For John that was not too high a price to pay. He took a hard line, advocating that Christians should at all costs keep themselves clean from the pollution of idolatrous images and an idolatrous system.

The mark is defined not only as the "name of the beast" but also as the "number of its name" (13:17). Then the Seer says that the number of the Beast conceals the name of a human being, and the number is 666 (13:18).

Endless speculation has surrounded this mysterious number almost from the first appearing of the book of Revelation. The Seer himself says that he is talking about a human being (13:18), but which human being? Every age has produced its own identification.

Each letter of the Hebrew and Greek alphabets carried a traditional, known numerical value. It happens that "Nero Caesar" in Hebrew letters = 666. But many other names are possible, if different values are assigned to the letters of different alphabets (Hebrew, Greek, English). And ingenuity is never in short supply. During the 1930s, for example, a political cartoon using the values A = 101, B = 102, C = 103 and so forth, mocked Hitler as the Beast.

The Seer himself had Nero or one of the other Roman emperors in mind. As the book of Revelation progresses, John's visions become ever more clearly anti-Roman. He fights not evil in general but Roman evil in particular, or evil incarnated in the Roman imperial system. Rome strutted on the stage of human history, boasting that its iron rule brought the benefactions of peace and plenty to the peoples of the earth. John's Revelation unmasks the pretensions of imperial Rome (and by extension every domination system), proclaiming that the downfall of Rome and not its continuation would yield divine blessings of peace and wholeness for a tortured cosmos.

The Antichrist

The name "Antichrist" never appears in the book of Revelation. In fact that word is used in very few biblical texts. The author of First John says that the future coming of "the Antichrist" is a common belief, but he shows no interest in that future advent. He declares that "many antichrists" are right now at work in the world (1 John 2:18). He uses the antichrist tradition to emphasize the seriousness of falling away from faith in Jesus as God's Son. The "antichrists" are lapsed Christians who now deny that Jesus is the Christ and say that Christ has not come in the flesh of Jesus (1 John 2:22; 4:3; 2 John 7; see Polycarp to the Philippians 7:1).

In early Christian times the Antichrist or Anti-Messiah was thought of as the last and ultimate agent of the devil, a completely evil human being (or demonic figure of superhuman proportions) who will lead one final assault on God and on God's Messiah in a vain effort to frustrate the establishing of the kingdom of God.

In some older traditions, predating the New Testament, a tyrant more terrible than any known so far is expected to raise his head and make war on God and the people of God in the end times. In Ezekiel 38–39 it is Gog of Magog (cf. Rev 20:7-10). In the Testaments of the Twelve Patriarchs the demonic figure Beliar will come to lead Israel astray (Test. Dan 5:10-

11; cf. Belial, the leader of the sons of darkness in the Dead Sea Scrolls). In Daniel 7, the Syrian King Antiochus IV is the tyrant behind the "little horn" arrogantly raging against the people of God.

In Mark's Gospel, Jesus warns about "false christs" (Mark 13:22) and, echoing Daniel 7, a "desolating sacrilege" (13:14). 2 Thessalonians names "the lawless one" and "one destined for destruction" (NRSV 2 Thess 2:3; RSV: "the man of lawlessness" and "the son of perdition") as figures of the end time.

From earliest times all these have been combined with features of the beast from the sea whose number is 666 (Rev 13), the one on whom the Harlot sits (Rev 17), to yield the traditional portrait of "the Antichrist."

Age after age Christians have struggled to apply these texts to their own particular situation. And they have recognized the Beast in whatever person or power they regarded as evil incarnate. So the Beast has been identified as Nero, Islam, Saladin, the pope, King George, Stalin, Hitler, and others.

Common today, especially among fundamentalists, is the notion that the Beast is the computer of the World Bank in Belgium or some other gigantic computer, and that the mark of the Beast is a computer chip that sinister powers are plotting to implant in our hand or forehead. What this new myth reveals is a widespread sense that we are losing our freedoms and that dark, mysterious forces are conspiring to gain control over every aspect of our lives.

In ancient numerology in general and in Revelation in particular, the number seven is the number of perfection. In ancient prophetic books called the Sybilline Oracles the name "Jesus" has the numerical value of 888. That signifies that Jesus surpasses even the perfect number 777. The number six may be a way of indicating something that tries desperately to mimic perfection but always falls short. So 666 (= "triple 6") may mean a completely bogus and inadequate leader, an absolutely evil opposite of the Lamb.

John's Apocalypse calls Christians today to prophetic criticism of our own political and social system. We must ask ourselves whether our commercial and political and social systems promote justice or oppression, life or violence. Liberationists say we need more than the mild rebukes of mainstream churches speaking from their comfortable positions inside the dominant system. They say we need the apocalyptic criticism of people who are not afraid to take their stand outside the system in solidarity with the poor and marginalized. Standing at the periphery, they say, we will see more clearly the nature of the beast.

John describes the two Beasts as the hands and mouth of the Dragon. The Dragon shares with them his own authority. Who can resist their power? (13:4). Very few, as it turns out.

As in previous woodcuts Dürer portrays people of all sorts and conditions as worshipers of the Beast. No kind or rank of humanity is immune to the blandishments. More than half of the woodcut is filled by the Beasts and their adoring adherents. The size of the space they occupy is an indication of their great success.

Time and the Cross *(13:5)*

As terrible as the power of the first Beast may be, the Seer reminds his readers that the Beast's authority is limited to "forty-two months" (13:5). We have seen that that is code language for a brief period of hardship limited by God's own decree (11:1, 19; 12:6). It designates the time of persecutions and distress allotted by God before the final overthrow of evil. In Rev 12:12-14, the heavenly voice itself interprets "a time and times and half a time" as "a short time." The Seer is echoing Jesus' own promise that God will shorten the final days of terror for the sake of the elect (Mark 13:20).

Dürer cannot exactly replicate the Seer's report about a chronological limitation on the Beast's power to persuade and conquer. But as an Artist he has other means at his disposal for making the same point. Close to the margin on the righthand side of Dürer's woodcut, one beastly head looks up and sees that it is about to be struck a mortal blow. The fact that an angel wields that sword means that the blow will come from God. Furthermore, Dürer's angel carries a cross over the left shoulder (compare woodcut 6) and has raised the sword in such a way that the sword is superimposed on the cross. The Artist means that the sword or power of the angel is the cross. The Cross of Jesus is the sign by which God and God's people conquer. They have conquered and they will conquer, not by might or wisdom of their own, but through the death and resurrection of Jesus (1 Cor 1–2).

And the Face of God

Dürer goes beyond John in offering still more signs of heavenly constraints on the power of the two beasts. He includes in his woodcut of Revelation 13 several images found only in other chapters of Revelation. So God, enthroned in the heavens (4:1-11; 14:3), occupies the apex and center of Dürer's woodcut. The face of Dürer's God is full of dignity and seems distorted, grimacing, almost crushed with an awful sadness at the Dragon's success in deceiving the world. Dürer has perfectly captured the Seer's own fundamental conviction. Both the Seer and the Artist insist that God rules invisibly but truly, even when the whole world goes astray.

The posture and gestures of Dürer's God in this woodcut are very much like those of the emperor in the first of the woodcuts. There the earthly emperor gave orders for the boiling of the Seer. Here God, looking unbearably sad, gives the command to destroy evil and to summon all humanity to a final rendering of accounts.

Chapter 15

Revelation 14:1-5

The New Song of the 144,000

Revelation 14 opens with a vision of the 144,000 redeemed, victorious in heaven, singing a new song before the heavenly throne, in the presence of the Lamb and of the four living creatures and the twenty-four elders (14:1-5). John continues the chapter with further visions of Seven Angels of judgment, beginning with God's judgment on Babylon and those who have the mark of the Beast. Finally the wine of God's wrath flows like a terrible river (14:6-20).

In his thirteenth woodcut Dürer concentrates on the opening vision of Revelation 14, and it seems as though he wanted to crowd all 144,000 saints into his picture. He portrays them with palm branches, symbols of victory, and their heads are tilted back so that they are looking up in a posture of adoration toward the Lamb. Dürer includes some features of the Seven Angels of judgment in his fourteenth woodcut.

The New Song of the 144,000
(Rev 14:1-5)

The one hundred and forty-four thousand appear twice in the book of Revelation. Previously the Seer reported that twelve thousand from each of the twelve tribes of Israel were sealed upon their foreheads and guarded from approaching terrors (Rev 7:1-8, woodcut 6).

The 144,000 redeemed are now introduced once more here, immediately following chapter 13, not as a mere continuation of chapter 13 but more as a response to it. The 144,000 represent all those who obey the call for endurance and faith issued by the Seer in the middle of chapter 13 (13:9-10). All these 144,000 refuse the mark of the Beast (13:16-18) and have on their foreheads the name of the Lamb and God's name (14:1).

The Seer hears the sound of angelic harpers. They lead the 144,000 in singing a "new song" before the throne and before the four living creatures and before the elders (see 5:9). No one can hear the celestial music and none can learn that new song except the 144,000 (14:2-3).

The 144,000 are now further described with terms that sound both patriarchal and ascetic. Those who are steadfast and faithful to God are called "virgins," and in the author's vision these are men, not women, because he defines these virgins as people "who never defiled themselves with women" (14:4).

I suppose it is just possible that the Seer is thinking literally of a band of super-Christians who have separated themselves so thoroughly from ordinary, secular life that they have renounced marriage and sexual relations. The Pastoral Epistles (1 and 2 Timothy and Titus) were probably written at roughly the same time as Revelation, and those letters had to defend marriage as an honorable vocation against certain Christians who denied the compatibility of marriage and the life of discipleship (1 Tim 4:3; see also 1 Cor 7). However, it is more likely that the Seer is speaking in figurative terms about all Christians, male and female, who are faithful to God.

All the way back to the prophet Hosea in the eighth century before Christ, a strong tradition spoke of infidelity to God as "adultery," and described loyalty to God in terms of the faithfulness of husband and wife.

For the Seer, infidelity to God was the great temptation and sin of the churches (2:14, 20). These spiritual "virgins" are pure and spotless. They were never guilty of any act of faithlessness toward God. And no lie was ever found in their mouth. The Seer uses purity and virginity as metaphors of their absolute and unyielding faithfulness towards God in the midst of a sometimes alluring, sometimes threatening environment.

Furthermore, abstaining from sexual relations for a set time before battle was part of the ritual preparation for Holy War in the Old Testament. The Seer believes that all Christians are called to be warriors in God's final attack on evil.

Dürer's Vision of Salvation

Dürer offers a collage of images as he works to communicate the Seer's intent. Within a large, central medallion, glowing like a halo, the Artist has placed the Lamb with seven eyes and seven horns, bearing a flag emblazoned with the insignia of the Cross. The Lamb stands on the rainbow of God's grace, and from his side a stream of blood spurts directly into a chalice held by one of the elders, pictured wearing the hat of a cardinal. This is the way Dürer interprets John's description of the 144,000 as people who "follow the Lamb wherever he goes" (14:4). The Lamb, of course, moved along the hard path leading directly to the cross. Peter once claimed that he would go wherever Jesus went, but Jesus responded that such following would be possible only "later," namely after Jesus' own death and resurrection (John 13:36-38).

In the Seer's view, those who follow the Lamb "wherever he goes" are especially the martyrs. But they include all who take up their cross and follow Jesus. Having followed the Christ on earth, they will follow "wherever he goes," and that includes following him through martyrdom right into the life of the world to come (cf. John 13:36-38).

Dürer has drawn the four living creatures (the Lion, the Ox, the Human Being, and the Eagle) inside smaller medallions in the space around the enthroned Lamb.

The Lamb and the four creatures in this woodcut seem, as elsewhere in the series, weakly drawn in contrast to the stronger portraits of humans and angels in Dürer's woodcuts.

John kneels on the hills of Patmos at the lower edge of the woodcut, while one of the twenty-four elders speaks to him across the great divide between heaven and earth. The power and majesty of heaven are pressing down and nearly shove the earthly realm with all its cares and temptations right out of this woodcut. Both Seer and Artist are successful in portraying the cosmic music of the heavenly throne room as an overwhelming reality.

The Seer had earlier described the great innumerable multitude as standing with palm branches in their hands, praising God and the Lamb (7:9-12). Revelation 14 says nothing of palm branches, but Dürer has combined elements of the two visions of the 144,000 (Rev 7 and 14) into this one woodcut.

All this is blessed assurance. In spite of the assaults of the Dragon and the Beasts, God will have the last word. History will end not in darkness but at the feet of the Creator. The saints are alerted that their faithful resistance is seen and valued by the Almighty. Otherwise, how could they stand firm in the plagues about to be unleashed?

Chapter 16

Revelation 14:6–16:21

Seven Angels of Judgment and Seven Angels with Seven Plagues

Seven Angels of Judgment
(Rev 14:6-20)

The Seer next reports seeing Seven Angels of judgment (14:6-20). Instead of devoting a separate woodcut to these seven, Dürer has borrowed a few details of their story and incorporated them into woodcut number 12. Here I offer a few summary statements on these Seven Angels.

The first three of the angels call the nations to "fear and glorify God alone" (14:7), announce the impending fall of "Babylon the great" (14:8, and see Rev 17–18), and threaten with the "wine of God's wrath" all who worship the Beast and bear his mark (14:9-11).

For the saints the message of these first three angels is a call for endurance. Their resistance is to be stiffened by their trust that God's all seeing eye notes their fidelity to the Lamb and will bless them with an everlasting blessing, never to be cancelled, not even by death (14:12-13). And God sees the evil of Babylon and is ready to topple that enemy of God's people.

Of the remaining four angels in John's vision, two hold sickles and two call to their angelic partners to use their sickles. The two with sickles then begin to harvest. One cuts wheat (14:16) and the other gathers grapes (14:18-19). Harvesting is an ancient biblical symbol of ingathering for judgment and salvation, also in the mouth of Jesus (Matt 9:37; 13:24-30). Sometimes harvest is an image full of joyful promise (John 4:35), and so here harvesting the wheat appears to mean gathering in the redeemed. In the immediately preceding context, the 144,000 redeemed are called "the firstfruits" (14:4), a harvest metaphor. However, the grape harvest spells judgment in the grimmest fashion. The grapes are thrown into the wine press of the wrath of God, and blood flows from the press, issuing in a fantastic river of blood four feet deep and two hundred miles long (14:20)!

In his woodcut devoted primarily to the beasts of Revelation 13, Dürer has drawn three angels not seven, but those three clearly represent all seven of the angels of Revelation 14. One strong angel kneeling at the upper left of Dürer's woodcut number 12 prays with folded hands, a second wearing the apron of a laborer grips a sickle, and a third flying through the sky on the right margin carries a cross and sword.

The Seer himself describes the fourth of the heavenly figures as having a human form. He is "like a son of man" or "like a human being" (14:14), sits on a white cloud, wears a golden crown and holds a sharp sickle.

One traditional interpretation of this figure insists that it is none other than the glorified Christ (1:13). Dürer, however, has chosen to set that golden crown on God's head and to place that sharp sickle into God's hand.

But it seems that the Seer himself intends us to understand this fourth figure in human-like form to be neither God nor Christ in glory but an angel. The Seer explicitly numbers the first three figures and calls them angels (14:8, 9). Then he breaks off the count when he comes to describe this fourth figure, this one whom he describes as being in form "like a human being." Human being is what "one like a son of a human being" means. The fact that John has failed to use the word "angel" for this fourth figure leads to a bit of confusion. Nevertheless, we are surely expected to understand all seven of these figures in chapter 14 as angels.

That these seven should be interpreted as a homogeneous group is confirmed by the fact that their actions parallel the breaking of the seven seals (Rev 6), the blasting of the seven trumpets (Rev 8–9), and the emptying of the seven bowls (Rev 15–16). Here in Revelation 14 the Seer is describing one more series of seven. These seven, like the sevens before and after them, are also agents of God. They are given dreadful work to accomplish, but all their workings are under God's control.

In Dürer's woodcut God holds in one hand a sickle and points with the other hand directly at the Beast. The angels flanking God, one praying and the other with a ready sickle, announce God's double judgment completely reversing the works of the Beast: terrible death for those to whom the Beast gives breath, blessed life for those whom the Beast causes to be slain.

The cross and sword of the third angel repeat the message of grace and judgment. With this woodcut Dürer portrays the fateful choices set before humankind in all the days before that dread announcement rings out from heaven, "Cut with your sickle and reap! The harvest is ripe!" (14:15).

Seven Angels with Seven Plagues
(Rev 15–16)

Entirely missing from Dürer's woodcuts is any representation of Revelation 15 or 16, with their vision of Seven Angels with Seven Bowls or Seven Plagues. He must have felt he could safely omit them, because they resemble the terrors accompanying the breaking of the seals in Revelation 6–7 (woodcuts 4 and 5) and the actions of the Seven Angels in Revelation 14 (preceding woodcut). Even closer are the parallels between the pouring out of the Seven Bowls in Revelation 15–16 and the blowing of the Seven Trumpets in Revelation 8 (woodcuts 7 and 8).

But we should not omit these chapters simply because Dürer does. They deserve at least a few lines, if for no other reason than the fact that only here in the entire Bible do we hear about the famous battle of Armageddon.

Another Portent *(15:1)*

This final series of seven disasters opens with the Seer exclaiming: "Then I saw another portent in heaven"

(15:1). Previously John had seen the "portent" or sign of the woman clothed with the sun (12:1) and the "portent" of the great red dragon (12:3). Now he sees another great portent: "seven angels with seven plagues" (15:1).

"Plagues" have been mentioned once or twice before in Revelation (9:18; 11:6) but the plagues of chapters 15 and 16 are described as "seven" in number, and they are further designated as "final" or the "last" (15:1, 6; see also 21:9). When these final plagues are poured out, God's wrath on human sinfulness will be exhausted (15:1). Then will come the dawn of the new creation.

The Song of Moses and of the Lamb *(15:2-4)*

Before the Seer utters another word about the angels or their plagues, he lifts our eyes to the heavenly throne room. The vision of heavenly reality, as often before (4:1-11; 8:2-5; 11:15-19; 14:1-5), interrupts scenes of otherwise unrelieved terror on earth. Heavenly visions offer a reading of events from God's point of view and strengthen readers for the shocks to come.

First (15:2) John sees all those who had conquered the Beast, and who had probably paid the price of martyrdom in the process, standing beside heaven's crystal sea (compare 4:6), singing "the song of Moses and of the Lamb" (15:3). Previously John had seen the 144,000 and heard them singing a "new song" before the throne (14:3). Now once more, in a parallel scene, he hears the redeemed chanting God's praises, grateful for the deeds of God and the ways of God and the name of God. They celebrate in advance that great day coming, when all nations will worship God who alone is holy (15:3-4). Earth may for a brief time resound with the sighs and groanings of the church and with the terror-stricken cries of the nations, as the plagues are unleashed. But God in heaven is and forever will be enthroned upon the songs of the redeemed (4:1–5:14; 7:12; 11:16-18).

Seven Golden Bowls *(15:5–16:1)*

Fortified by the vision of the joyous liturgy in heaven, we may be able to endure what follows. Seven Angels emerge from the heavenly temple. One of the four living creatures gives to the Seven Angels seven golden bowls, ominously described as "full of God's wrath." Immediately the temple seems to explode with smoke and fire, like Mount Sinai when Moses went up to talk with God (Exod 24; cf. 1 Kgs 8:10; Isa 6:4). No one can approach the heavenly sanctuary until God's wrath has burned itself out and the Seven Plagues are past (15:5-8).

God, wrapped in a mantle of mystery, gives the signal for the Seven Angels to pour out the Seven Bowls (16:1). Like the angels with the Seven Trumpets (8:2–9:21), these Seven Angels (15:1–16:21) unleash terrors reminiscent of the ten plagues scourging Egypt in the time of Moses and the Exodus (Exod 7–12; seven or eight plagues in Ps 78:42-51; 105:26-36).

The Judgments of God *(16:2-11)*

The first four plagues are directed especially at those who bear the mark of the Beast, worship its image, curse God and oppress the people of God (16:2-9). Like the first four of the Seven Trumpets, the bowls of the first four angels strike in turn the earth (16:2), the sea (16:3), fresh waters (16:4-7), and the chief heavenly body, the sun (16:8-9).

The "angel of the waters" (16:5), that is, the angel controlling all of earth's waters, causes the water to turn to blood (Exod 7:17-21). Then the angel chants a kind of war cry that makes it sound as though God has thrown a temper tantrum and has lashed out in vengeance at those who have shed "the blood of saints and prophets." And yet a few verses farther on, the fourth angel announces that these plagues are designed to drive the peoples of the earth not to bitterness or despair but to repentance (16:9).

The fifth plague strikes directly at the "throne of the beast," plunging its whole kingdom into darkness and pain. But still the minions of the beast do not repent (16:10-11).

Armageddon *(16:12-16)*

The sixth plague dries up the River Euphrates, ancient boundary between Parthia (Persia) and the Roman Empire, paving the way for an eastern invasion. The action parallels that of the sixth trumpet, which permitted a terrible horde of invaders to cross the Euphrates (9:13-21). In a further grotesque image, the Seer describes "three unclean spirits like frogs" emerging from the mouths of the Dragon, the Beast and the "false prophet." "False prophet" is another name for the second Beast of Revelation 13 (see 13:11-18). These "three frogs" are demonic spirits, who by their words and impressive signs induce the kings of the world to rise up against God.

So John pictures the unholy trinity making foul, croaking noises in contrast to the psalms and anthems of the heavenly choir. Their demonic croaking summons all the kings of the earth to gather for war against God at the fabled battleground called "Armageddon" (16:12-16; "Armageddon" in KJV and RSV; "Harmagedon" in NRSV).

The name Armageddon or Harmagedon seems to mean "Mount Megiddo." Megiddo was a fortified city commanding a strategic pass through which a major north-south highway ran. King Josiah led the forces of Judah in a disastrous battle against the Egyptian Pharaoh Neco at Megiddo (2 Kgs 23:29-30). Armageddon burned a scar in the Israelite mind and lived in biblical memory as an image of futile warfare (2 Chron 35:20-25; cf. Judg 5:19).

After six bowls of wrath we have every right to expect the Seer to describe finally how God overwhelms the rebellious hosts, but once again John stops short. He notes only that the kings assemble their armies. John seems to picture them milling about, imagining that they command the battlefield. Their horses and chariots are ready. Their armor and weapons are sharp and sparkling. They can almost taste victory. But the day does not belong to them. Rather it is "the great day of God Almighty" (16:14), and the "wrath" of God is about to burst upon them. (See what happens at the opening of the sixth seal in 6:12-17). They feel supremely confident, oblivious to the fact that they stand unclothed and naked before God (16:15).

The Seer brings us to Armageddon but once again delays. He will describe the world's final battle and its outcome later, in Rev 19:11-21. But first he turns our eyes to the seventh plague.

The Seventh Bowl *(16:17-21)*

The seventh angel pours out the contents of the seventh bowl, and a loud voice from the temple, indeed from the throne itself cries out, "It is done, finished, ended!" (v. 17). Can this be any other than the voice of God? Lightning flashes, thunder peals, and great quakes convulse the earth, flattening the tallest mountains and swallowing every island. Huge hailstones, each weighing a hundred pounds, fall to earth with crushing force. But sadly the Seer reports that the plague of hail leads people only to cursing and not to repentance.

The Seer uses the language of theophany, of God's bursting forth in invincible self-disclosure (see Exod 19:16-19 and Heb 12:18-24). The seventh bowl seems to bring us all the way to the end, and yet once more it is not the end. The Seer declares that God's fury is set to break out against the rebellious cities of the earth and especially against "great Babylon" (16:17-21). The identity of "Babylon" and its fate occupy the next two chapters of Revelation (17–18).

Chapter 17

Revelation 17:1–19:10

Babylon, the Mother of All Whores

An angel shows John a woman with the mysterious name "Babylon" written on her forehead. She is described as "the Mother of all Whores" (17:5). At first we are told that the woman sits on a scarlet beast with seven heads (17:3), the same beast which the Dragon summoned up out of the depths of the sea at the beginning of chapter 13. But then John proceeds to tell us that the woman is a city built on seven hills (17:9). This city must be Rome, even though the name "Rome" never actually appears in Revelation. The woman-city, enemy of the people of God, may boast of being "eternal," but she is overthrown "in a single hour" (18:10, 17).

In his fourteenth woodcut Dürer describes Babylon as whore (Rev 17), tells the story of her fall (Rev 18), and shows the victorious Christ descending out of the clouds, at the head of heaven's armies (Rev 19:11-16).

Babylon, the Mother of All Whores
(Rev 17:1–19:10)

As John nears the end of his book, he offers visions of two cities, one holy and the other unholy. He reports his visions in carefully crafted language so that readers will see parallels and make comparisons. First he speaks of the unholy city to which he gives the symbolic name "Babylon" (Rev 17:1–19:10). Then he reports his vision of the holy city, which he calls "New Jerusalem" (21:9–22:11).

The two visions are structured in similar fashion: (1) Both visions open with a scene in which one of the Seven Angels with the Seven Bowls says to John, "Come, I will show you!" (17:1-3; 21:9-10). (2) Then the angel carries John off "in the spirit" (see 1:10), taking him to the wilderness in one case (17:3) and to a high mountain (21:10) in the other. (3) What is shown to him in the first vision is a woman, a great whore or harlot (chapter 17), and in the second he sees a pure bride (chapter 21). (4) The angel explains to John that these women he sees are two cities and offers detailed descriptions of the unholiness of the one and the holiness of the other. (5) At the conclusion of each vision, the angel pronounces a blessing (19:9; 22:7). (6) When John falls down to worship the angel, he is chastised and told to worship God alone (19:10; 22:8-9).

The similar treatment indicates that John invites us to compare and contrast the Whore/Babylon (chapter 17) and the Holy Bride/New Jerusalem (chapters 21–22). These two women or cities are two human communities: the people caught up in idolatrous worship of the Beast, and the people of God. These two embody two divergent sets of commitments and hopes, and they symbolize two radically different destinies for human beings.

The Great Whore (17:3-6)

The angel summons John to see "the great whore with whom the kings of the earth committed fornication" (17:1-2). Carried away by the angel, the Seer beholds the whore, in fact "the mother of all whores" (17:5), sitting on a scarlet beast. The Beast is covered with names insulting to God, and it has seven heads and ten horns (17:3). The seven heads are seven Roman emperors, while the ten horns are allied kings of subject peoples. This beast is none other than the first of the two Beasts of Revelation 13, summoned up by the Dragon from the sea.

John offers two different visions of the Roman Empire. In chapter 13 he views it in terms of its overwhelming military power and speaks of it as making war on the saints (13:7). Here in chapter 17 he portrays Rome not as conquering and killing but as seducing, like a whore. Of course the two images, Rome as conqueror and Rome as seductress, are closely related. The Roman system with its dazzling, alluring wealth rides on the back of Rome's military might. In its dealings with the peoples of the world, Rome compels and Rome seduces. Here in chapter 17 and in 18 John concentrates on the seductive allure of Rome and the attractiveness of its economic system which brought prosperity to many.

In John's vision the whore is clothed magnificently, and she holds in her hand a wonderful gold cup, but it is full of impurities (17:4), brimming with the blood of slaughtered saints and martyrs (17:4). The woman teeters unsteadily, and John says that she is "drunk on the blood of saints and witnesses to Jesus" (17:6). Is this a reference to the martyrdoms in Rome in the year 64 under Emperor Nero?

The Mystery of the Woman (17:7-18)

The whore bears the name "Babylon" (17:5), and at the close of the chapter John offers a very large clue by saying that the whore is "a city" which rules over kings and kingdoms (17:18). Everything seems so precise and definite, but what exactly is meant by this "Babylon"?

Historical Babylon, Israel's ancient foe, was a city "seated by many waters" (17:1). Built on the Euphrates River (9:14; 16:12), ancient Babylon was watered by an intricate network of canals. But the Seer is using the name Babylon symbolically. He calls it a "mystery" (17:5, 7). All indications are that he means the city of Rome, called "Babylon" also in 1 Peter 5:13.

Like ancient Babylon, Rome in John's day was the center of a vast empire and lorded it over the kings of the earth. Like Babylon, Rome sat "on many waters" (17:1). Babylon had its complex web of canals fed by the Euphrates, and Rome ruled all the lands ringing the Mediterranean and was located at the center of a vast system of land routes and sea lanes.

The Seer helps us to crack the code of the mystery of the name "Babylon" by saying that the city was situated on seven hills (17:9). In ancient times that phrase, "on seven hills," was a common adjective for Rome.

One reason why the Seer called Rome "Babylon" was because Rome, like Babylon, had attacked the holy city and destroyed the temple of God. Babylon did it in 586 B.C. Rome did it in A.D. 70, within the lifetime of the Seer.

Rome was deeply repulsive to the Seer, and not only because of its emperor worship and the cult of the goddess Roma. Rome conquered tribes and nations on its borders, incorporated them into the empire, and then proceeded to squeeze them dry, sucking up their resources for the benefit of the emperor and the small upper class of Roman elites. To John the imperial city of Rome was an earthy "Babylon," dark and alluring counterpart of the Heavenly Jerusalem (Rev 21). With its glitter and power, Babylon-Rome was not just a cruel conqueror. It was also "harlot," seducing populations, including Christians, to seek her favors. The Seer accuses Rome of turning the heads of rulers and merchants, priests and soldiers, artisans and housewives away from God toward the worship of human wealth and human power.

Dürer's Babylon

Dürer pictures the whore as dressed in the finery of Venice, since in his day, late in the fifteenth century, Venice with its celebrated canals and its great commercial empire, its arrogance and elegance, seemed to him to be one current incarnation of seductive "Babylon." Dürer does not portray canals or rivers but does picture the scarlet beast on which the woman sits as a watery monster slouching up out of abyss (17:3, 8; 10:7; cf. 13:1).

Here again, as in the preceding woodcut, a chalice holds center stage in Dürer's composition. In the woodcut of the 144,000 (Rev 14) Dürer pictures the cup of the church's Holy Communion, the cup of Christ's

triumphant sacrifice, the chalice of God's astonishing grace, filled with the precious blood of the Lamb. Here the woman described by the Seer as a whore, indeed as "the mother of whores" (17:5), holds a jeweled cup full of abominations and impurities, namely the blood or murder of the saints. Hers is a chalice of murder.

So the one cup says, "Life for God's saints!" The other, "Death to the people of God!" The one proclaims God's own self-giving. The other is all self-indulgence and rebellion against God.

In his woodcut on Babylon-Rome, Dürer portrays the same cast of characters as in his first woodcut. Here the emperor with his ermine collar has his back turned to the viewer, but the faces as well as the costumes of others are readily seen, and it is easy to identify the same people in both woodcuts.

For a short time Babylon-Rome enjoys the support of the beast. The whore sits on the Beast, and the Beast "carries her" (17:7). And yet the alliance is unstable. The heads and horns of the Beast are kings and rulers allied to Rome (17:9-12). They support the woman for a time, but soon enough they turn on her in hatred, strip her naked, and devour her (17:16). The coalition of evil powers is self-destructive.

Fallen, Fallen Is Babylon the Great (Rev 18:1-24)

The Seer records a series of poems, usually called taunt songs and dirges, marking in advance the fall of Babylon, as though she were already dead (18:1-24). Her demise is that certain.

A Mighty Angel *(18:1-3)*

At the top of Dürer's woodcut a mighty angel with one hand gestures to God's people and with the other summons them to behold Babylon's fate. The angel cries, "Fallen, fallen is Babylon the great!" The once great city will become a ghost town because of its immorality and idolatry.

Another Voice *(18:4-8)*

A voice of warning rings out, summoning God's people to separate themselves from that doomed city and all it stands for. This is a central theme in John's Revelation. His great fear is that the loyalty of his Christian congregations is fatally divided between Christ and Caesar. He warns them that being friends of the whore Babylon is just begging to be destroyed with her. He cries out to readers to remember that "she will be burned up in fire!" (18:8). Dürer echoes the Seer's vision by showing the city at the edge of the water being consumed in flames.

Kings Weep and Merchants Mourn *(18:9-19)*

Puppet kings, allies of the great city, weep and wail to see Babylon-Rome fall. They are astonished that the end came so quickly. All roads and all sea-lanes led to Rome, carrying the wealth of the provinces to the capital city. Merchants and traders, sailors and shipmasters remember fondly all the luxury goods required by Rome's extravagance and how that need for luxury had made them wealthy.

The list of imported goods (18:11-13) is testimony to Rome's voracious appetite. The list of twenty-eight items begins with gold and silver and climaxes with a reminder that Rome trafficked not only in things but also in slaves, in human beings. In fact the prosperity of Rome depended on the oppression of vast masses of conquered peoples. The emperor sat at the apex of a great pyramid. A rich and powerful minority enjoyed immense wealth, while millions were consigned to lives of desperate poverty and degradation.

In its propaganda Rome described itself as "the eternal city." But now kings and rulers, merchants and shipmasters lamented together, "In one hour all this wealth has been laid waste" (18:8, 16-17, 19). They had grown fat in their alliances with the city, and now they throw dust on their heads, mourning at the smoke of her burning.

A Great Millstone *(18:20-24)*

John sees a mighty angel throw a great millstone into the sea (18:21). Dürer pictures that angel, ready to throw the millstone. The Seer describes the angel as crying out, "Babylon the great city is about to be thrown down" (18:21). The angel exults at how the city, once humming and buzzing with the sounds of every conceivable form of human activity, will fall into an eerie silence. No more music. No more sounds of grinding mills or hammering craftsmen. No more laughter of bride and groom. And no more light. Only silence and gloom. That is the fate of the idolatrous, oppressor city.

John concludes his chapter with a call to God's people. They must not join in the general lamentation at the fall of the unholy city. They should rather rejoice. The destruction of Babylon-Rome is God's judgment on an empire that prospered while drinking the blood of prophets and saints and so many others besides (18:20, 24).

The Marriage of the Lamb *(19:1-10)*

Earth laments but heaven rejoices at the fall of Babylon. A multitude of the heavenly host breaks into song, praising God in a pair of alleluias for judging "the great whore who corrupted the earth with her fornication," her alluring and idolatrous liaisons (19:1-3). Then to that mighty chorus the twenty-four elders and the four living creatures add their "Amen" and "Hallelujah" (19:4).

A voice from the throne summons all God's servants to join in the praise. The Seer hears sounds as of great crowds of people, like the roaring of many waters or the mighty clapping of thunder (19:6). The whole universe breaks out in praise of God whose hour of victory has come.

Judgment on Babylon clears the way for the marriage of the Lamb. The great whore is destroyed, and the Lamb's Bride has made herself ready. She is clothed in her wedding finery. To make sure we understand the meaning of the Bride's clothing, "fine linen, bright and pure," the Seer tells us that her wedding gown consists of "the righteous deeds of the saints" (19:8). The persevering people of God wear the white robes of faith and fidelity (3:5; 6:11; 7:9, 14; 16:15) and will be presented to the Lamb, as bride to husband (2 Cor 11:2).

Then the angel tells the Seer to write, "Blessed are those who are invited to the Lamb's wedding feast!" At the end, beyond all sadness, comes the glad union of the faithful with the Lamb.

Chapter 18

Revelation 19:11–22:21

Binding of Satan and the New Jerusalem

After Christ's victory in the great battle of Armageddon (16:12-16 and 19:19-21), the Dragon (the devil) is bound and cast into the pit for a thousand years (20:1-3). Peace reigns on earth during that whole millennium (20:4-6). But then at the end of the thousand years, the devil is released and mounts one final frantic assault on God and the people of God (20:7-10). The devil is instantly defeated, and all appear before the judgment seat of God (20:11-15). At last John sees a new heaven and a new earth, and the New Jerusalem descends from God out of heaven as an eternal habitation for the people of God (Rev 21–22).

Dürer's fifteenth and final woodcut omits much. He has already treated the descent of Christ in his fourteenth woodcut. Here in this last woodcut Dürer sums up the goal of the whole biblical drama in two scenes.

In the lower portion of this woodcut Dürer pictures a marvelously serene angel bending to the task of ridding the world of the dragon. Carrying a great key, a length of iron chain and a huge padlock, the angel has seized the Dragon and is in the process of stuffing him down into the bottomless pit (20:1-3).

The wings of that victorious angel are drawn by Dürer in such a way that they form a kind of shield, a divinely ordained barrier between the pit and the Dragon below and the New Jerusalem above. The devil's reign is finished. The door to the abyss is about to clank shut over him, absolutely removing him from any further influence on earth.

In the upper portion of his woodcut Dürer pictures the angel pointing out the wonders of the New Jerusalem to John, who stands, gazing awestruck at God's handiwork.

Binding of Satan and the New Jerusalem
(Rev 19:11–22:21)

In this final section of his book the Seer offers a kaleidoscope of images. He sees a Rider named "Word of God" descending on a white horse from heaven at the head of a great host arrayed in white (19:11-16), a gruesome supper of God in which birds eat the flesh of fallen armies (19:17-18), the defeat of the Beast and the False Prophet (19:19-21), the Binding of Satan (20:1-3), the Thousand Year Reign of Christ (20:4-6), the Defeat of Satan (20:7-10) and the Final Judgment (20:11-15). Then in the last of his visions John sees the first heaven and the first earth vanishing away, and he beholds the descent of the New Jerusalem to the new earth (21–22).

With these final visions John is not necessarily describing events that he expects to happen one after the other in strict chronological sequence. John's goal is doxology, not chronology. Each vision is an epiphany, a great flash that lights up the dark landscape of our existence. Each opens a different window onto some aspect of the future toward which history is rushing.

Dürer was confronted with hard choices as he tried to organize his woodcuts. He decided to include some of John's visions and he has excluded others. The Artist has already incorporated one of John's visions elsewhere, showing the Rider on the white horse coming from heaven (19:11-16), in his woodcut of the fall of Babylon. A few additional words on that woodcut are in order here.

The Rider on the White Horse *(19:11-16)*

At the extreme upper left of Dürer's woodcut on the fall of Babylon, the heavens have opened and the armies of heaven, dressed in white linen, stream down like sands in an hourglass. They are led by "a white horse and one seated on it." John says the rider bears the names "Faithful and True" (19:11), "The Word of God" (19:13), and "King of kings and Lord of lords" (19:16; cf. 17:14 and Dan 2:47). Obviously, this rider is Christ arriving from heaven to rout all the enemies of God's people.

In Dürer's woodcut the downward motion of the heavenly host seems to be aimed directly at the harlot. In John's book, however, the harlot has already been vanquished by this time, and heaven's armies are gathering for the final battle against the beast and the false prophet and all their followers (19:19-21).

Dürer's Christ wears wonderful protective armor and looks exactly like an imperial general. However, John says that Christ wears not armor but a garment dipped in blood (19:13). In this context that "blood" (19:13) does not sound like the blood of the Lamb given and shed for all in an act of nearly incomprehensible forgiveness. It is more like the blood shed by a tough martyr who summons others to a similar hard choice (see 1:5-6).

Neither here nor elsewhere in Revelation does the Seer picture a very pacific Christ. John's Christ wields as weapons a sharp sword and a rod of iron (19:15). This Messiah is one who prosecutes with utmost seriousness the "war" between Christ and culture. He leads his people in battle, takes no prisoners, and gains a costly victory. And yet his name is "The Word of God," and his "sword" issues from his mouth and is his word (19:15, 21; cf. 1:16). And the Seer believes that his own words of prophetic testimony are Christ's sword, cutting at the enemies of God, inside and outside of the Christian community.

Note how in Dürer's woodcut, Christ's sword is aimed directly at one of the heads of the Beast. That head looks up in astonishment and unbelief at its impending fate.

The Great Supper of God *(19:17-18)*

The Seer then reports a gruesome scene. It is not found in any of Dürer's woodcuts. The Seer reports "an angel standing on the sun" (19:17), summoning all the carrion birds to gather for an awful feast. The enemies of God lie slaughtered on a vast battlefield. The angel calls upon crows and vultures to "eat the flesh" of the kings and captains, of the horses and riders and of all the rebellious hordes who made war on God. "Eat their flesh," cries the angel, and so make the earth clean.

This bizarre feast, foreshadowed by Ezekiel (39:17-20), is a terrible contrast with the wedding feast of the Lamb (19:9). And it announces in advance the aftermath of the great and final clash of arms known as "the Battle of Armageddon" (16:12-16).

The Beast and False Prophet Are Defeated *(19:19-21)*

John now sees the Beast and the kings of the earth preparing their armies to fight against the rider on the white horse and his heavenly host. John never describes this final conflict, this "Battle of Armageddon" (16:12-16). He simply reports how the armies gather and then notes the result of their warfare. The two beasts summoned up by the Dragon back in chapter 13 are fully and finally vanquished. Here, instead of being called "the first Beast" and "a second Beast" as earlier, they are now called "the Beast and the false prophet" (19:20). Together they are thrown into the lake of fire, forever removed from any further possibility of deceiving or injuring God's people.

So the "sword" that issues from the mouth of the mounted Rider whose name is "The Word of God" vanquishes all the enemies of God (19:21). The old has passed away. The Seer and the Artist are ready now to concentrate all their power on describing the new.

The Binding of Satan and the Kingdom of a Thousand Years *(20:1-6)*

Dürer drastically abbreviates Revelation 20–22, summing up their several visions in two powerful scenes. In this final woodcut Dürer concentrates all his artistry on depicting two complementary events of the end time: the lockout of the Dragon on the one hand, and the gates of the New Jerusalem flung wide open to the faithful on the other hand.

With his artistic abbreviation, Dürer stands in considerable tension with the Seer whose words he otherwise so wonderfully portrays in this woodcut. The actual text of Revelation 20–22 is too complex to be captured in any single woodcut. And it is far too rich to be summarized adequately in any brief paragraph, but we need to take account of some of the details of the Seer's text which have been omitted or altered by the Artist.

The Seer tells how an angel seizes the Dragon, throws him into the "abyss" or "bottomless pit" and

seals it over him (20:1-3). The pit or abyss is bottomless, but it is not endless, for the Seer says the Dragon will be locked up, not forever, but for "a thousand years" (20:2, 3, 4, 5, 7). At the start of that millennium, the martyred saints come to life and reign with Christ throughout that holy and peaceful thousand years. These are people who have not worshiped the Beast and have not received his mark on their foreheads or hands.

Satan Loosed and Doomed *(20:7-10)*

In his vision John sees all the way to the end of the millennium. Then, mysteriously, that old dragon Satan will be released for a brief moment, allowed to flex his muscles one last time, mounting yet one more rebellion against God, one last assault upon the people of God. John sees an army, numerous as the sands of the sea, marching up against the saints and the holy city. Ready for prolonged warfare, that army will however be destroyed in the twinkling of an eye by fire from heaven. Then at last the Dragon, the deceiver of humankind, will be thrown into the lake of fire. John writes as though the binding of Satan and the final defeat of Satan are two events separated by a thousand years. Dürer portrays Satan's ultimate defeat in a single dramatic scene. Satan is undone in the twinkling of an eye.

The Millennium

All Christian interpreters, from fundamentalist to liberationist, find common ground in viewing the Seer's vision of a messianic kingdom of a thousand years as a rich and potent symbol promising special rewards for the truly faithful. But then comes the parting of the ways.

Fundamentalists and the Millennium

Fundamentalists read Revelation 20 as a prediction of a future kingdom on earth to be ruled by Jesus Christ when he comes in glory to crush evil and establish righteousness. All the saints of God from ages past will be raised up to enjoy the millennial kingdom. Revelation singles out for special mention the "tribulation saints," those Israelites and Gentiles who were martyred during the tribulation because they refused to worship the Beast. Nevertheless the phrase "first resurrection" (Rev 20:5) describes the resurrection of all the faithful to newness of life. The "second resurrection" at the end of the thousand years will be the resurrection of the wicked to judgment.

Fundamentalists believe that all the prophecies of Scripture will find literal fulfillment and the details of that fulfillment will unfold according to a scheme made famous in the Scofield reference Bible and popularized in books by authors like Hal Lindsey and Tim Lahaye.

In that scheme Jerusalem will serve as capital of the millennial kingdom. Injustice and oppression will vanish. Wars between nations will be a thing of the past. The lion will literally lie down with the lamb as the earth enjoys the peace intended by God at creation. Plants will yield abundant harvests. People will have dozens of children and generation after generation of grandchildren and great grandchildren. Those who entered the millennium as children may well live for hundreds of years. Children born during the millennium will live all the way to its end.

According to this scheme of things, as the end of the millennium draws near, many on earth will never have decided for Christ and will not be true believers at all. Others will simply have grown complacent over the thousand years. They will make easy prey for the Dragon who will be released from the pit at the end of the thousand years and will lead one last doomed rebellion against God.

At one time fundamentalists criticized churchly involvement in social and political action. They regarded those involvements as misguided human efforts to create the millennium, a task which only God can accomplish. However, in the past quarter century fundamentalists and other conservative Christians have begin to move out more confidently into the public sphere, pressing in robust political fashion for their social and moral positions. They wrestle as all Christians do with the mystery of the connection between divine and human activity.

The Mainline and the Millennium

For hundreds of years mainline interpreters have followed St. Augustine in taking the millennium to symbolize the whole time of the church beginning with the Christ event (the life, death, and resurrection of Jesus), a period of time to be concluded by Christ's second coming and the last judgment.

This view sees the binding of Satan (Rev 20:2) in the earthly work of Jesus (see Mark 3:27; Luke 10:18). Christians at their baptism experience "the first resurrection" (Rev 20:5; Eph 2:1-10). Loosed from Satan's tyrannical grip, they rise up from the waters of baptism to begin living their lives under Christ's dominion as citizens of heaven (Phil 3:20). By the power of the Holy Spirit, they are able to resist Satan's unholy power and begin living the "millennial" life. As members of a new, alternative community, citizens of the new Israel, they join in heralding the news of Christ's triumph over Satan (evangelism). And they commit themselves to doing deeds of loving kindness, as they attempt to set up on the earth visible signs of the real but hidden reign of Christ and of God.

In other words, many in the mainstream do not take Revelation 20 as prophesying some future binding of Satan, followed by a literal millennium after which will come a last battle and ultimate defeat of Satan, climaxing in a future last judgment. Instead they read this chapter as offering a visionary perspective on what is always happening in human history since "Satan" was "bound" by Christ's life and death and resurrection.

Liberationists and the Millennium

Liberationists reject fundamentalistic literalism. To liberationists it seems that the fundamentalists read biblical prophecy as fortune-telling and date-setting. When fundamentalists are not waiting passively for God to act, they easily lapse into uncritical identification of American interests with God's own program.

Liberationists see the conservative, evangelical side of the Christian mainstream wasting its energy on strategies for getting rid of personal sinfulness in order to avoid the last judgment. And they see liberal elements of the mainstream offering mere tokens of sympathy to the poor while continuing to live lives of middle class comfort, blind to the monstrosities of the domination system. To liberationists it seems that the mainstream, very much like the fundamentalists, is captive to the dominant culture. In the view of liberationists, the mainstream fails to grasp the corporate and political dimensions of the message of the prophets and of Jesus himself.

Liberationists see in the thousand-year reign of Christ not a future period of history but a potent symbol of the glorious transformation of the world toward which God is wooing and enabling us every day. The millennium is a powerful vision meant to steel us for the struggle against the idolatry and oppressions of empires, including the American empire. It represents the goal for which we are to labor, pulling us like a powerful magnet toward the establishing of God's reign on earth. The picture of the millennial kingdom urges us to resist the dominant economic and social and political culture, enables us to conquer our fear of reprisal, and inspires us to live without self-pity or dogmatism while filling us with a spirit of hope and joy.

The Last Judgment *(20:11-15)*

Universal resurrection and final judgment follow swiftly on the last rebellion. John sees "a great white throne and One sitting on it." All the dead wake from their slumbers and stand around the throne. Books are opened, and all are judged "according to their works" (cf. Rom 2:6). Their deeds reveal whether they belong to God or the Dragon, to Christ or the Beast.

Death and Hades are consigned to the lake of fire together with all whose names are not found in the book of life (20:14-15). So finally all opposition to God's gracious sovereignty simply ceases to exist. But Revelation does not end with a vision of God sitting on a great white throne amid eerie solitude and silence. The history of the universe does not end with pictures of fire and devastation.

A New Heaven and a New Earth *(21:1-8)*

After all his images of catastrophe, rebellion, and judgment, the Seer is overwhelmed with a vision of an altogether splendid "new heaven and new earth" (21:1). John sees the holy city, new Jerusalem, descending to the new earth from God out of heaven, like a bride moving down the aisle to meet her husband (21:2). This city is the polar opposite of harlot Babylon (Rev 17).

And John hears the voice of God, full of grace and compassion, coming to dwell in the midst of humankind and promising to wipe the tears from every eye and to heal all pain and sorrow (21:3-4). Indeed, the one who sits upon the throne declares, "I am making all things new" (21:5).

Who inhabits the new city? Who enjoys God's presence? God, who is Alpha and Omega (21:6; cf. 1:8), welcomes all "the victors" (20:7), who have conquered the dark powers organized in opposition to God. John lists the kinds of people excluded from the new city, and his list is a summary of everything he despises beginning with cowards and the disloyal. That is a sharp warning to Christians who are inclined to go along with the dominant culture, fearful of losing comfort and privilege. In John's mind they are finally in the same category as murderers and fornicators (21:8).

The New Jerusalem *(21:9–22:5)*

In the upper portion of his woodcut Dürer pictures the scene which now follows in the Seer's report. One of the Seven Angels who once held bowls full of wrath carries the Seer to a great, high mountain and with a gesture of invitation, the opposite of the Dragon's harsh exile, points to the holy city, New Jerusalem (21:9).

Like a Bride *(21:1-27)*

What Dürer pictures, however, is not exactly the fabled city of the book of Revelation. The Seer speaks in stunning terms of a city wholly other than any earthly city. It shines with the glory of God and has the radiance of jewels and the clarity of crystal (21:11). Its twelve gateways, three on each of its four sides, are inscribed with the names of the twelve tribes of Israel, and its twelve foundations bear the names of the twelve apostles of the Lamb (21:12-14).

The angel talking to John measures the new city (cf. 11:1-2), and all its dimensions are multiples of the number 12. The city has twelve gates and twelve foundations (21:12-14). Like the ancient Holy of Holies (1 Kgs 6:20) the Seer's New Jerusalem is a perfect cube. The underlying Greek text of Revelation says that it stretches "12,000 stadia" (= about 1,500 miles) in length, 12,000 in width, and 12,000 in height (21:16). The wall that surrounds the city is 144 (12 x 12) cubits high (21:17).

The number 12 and its multiples (12; 24; 144; 12,000; 144,000) seem always to occur in contexts describing God's people. All these measurements involving the number twelve, the number of the people of God, signal that this new city is a splendid new habitation for a splendid new people.

Its twelve gates are never shut, because no evil menaces the city. The new city is safe and stands open in every direction. Therefore all the nations, north and south and east and west (Luke 13:29; Matt 8:11), may freely enter and dwell there (21:24-26).

The city wears more gems than any bride. Its twelve foundations are bejeweled, the twelve gates of the city are twelve pearls, and the main street of the city is paved with purest gold (21:21).

The new city has no temple because God and the Lamb are all the temple it needs (in contrast with Ezek 40–48). And the city has no need of sun or moon, for God is its light and its glory, and its lamp is the Lamb (21:22-23). Nations and kings, finally enlightened by the glory of God, contribute their glory to the new city, fulfilling old prophecy (21:24-27; Isa 60).

The Tree of Life *(22:1-5)*

So far the city that comes down from God out of heaven sounds cold as a diamond and hard as steel, sterile and unyielding. But then as his visions continue, the Seer begins to describe the city in warmer terms. He sees it as a renewed Garden of Eden. The Seer is shown "the river of the water of life, bright as crystal," springing forth from the throne of God and the Lamb in the heart of the city (22:1-2). And he sees "the tree of life" whose leaves are like aloes, for the healing of the nations. That fabulous tree bears twelve kinds of fruit, yielding a different kind each month of the year (22:2). So the new city both perfectly shelters and perfectly nourishes all who dwell there (cf. 7:16-17).

Dürer's City and the Seer's

Dürer's New Jerusalem is less awesome but more charming and inviting than the Seer's. Dürer has drawn a scrubbed and prosperous German town. If you look closely you can see a welcoming angel at each portal and on each tower, poised and ready to receive the saints of God (21:12). But Revelation contains much that Dürer had to omit or chose to omit, as he translated the words of the Seer into images made by spreading ink onto carved wooden panels.

Whatever tensions there may be between the Seer's words and the Artist's images, both Seer and Artist depict life in the present time all the way to the end as a struggle, and the struggle has many dimensions. It is not enough to define it only as a clash between social and economic classes or between families or clans or tribes or nations. Behind all the historic and ongoing struggles of humankind is the ancient warfare between good and evil, between God and Satan. Both the Seer and the Artist celebrate the outcome of that warfare ahead of time as the total victory of God when they portray the casting of the Dragon into the abyss and the triumphant descent to earth of the New Jerusalem, all purity and peace.

The final chapters of the Seer's book of Revelation and Dürer's last woodcut are celebrations, and they are

testimony. They bear witness that the fiery pit and the New Jerusalem are not just outcomes or conclusions but choices set before humankind. Artist and Seer are crying out to their viewers and readers to be faithful to God and the Lamb. The struggle is hard, but the faithful must remember that not even death can conquer them. They will dwell with God in everlasting bliss. But the cowardly, the faithless, and the polluted will be forever excluded from God's new city.

Dürer's first woodcut depicts earth alone, with John squatting in a cauldron of oil in the presence of the emperor seated on his royal throne. The second woodcut shows heaven alone, with the Christ-figure high and lifted up with heaven's double rainbow as his throne. Every other woodcut shows both earth and heaven, revealing the terrible discord between earthly and heavenly governments. Now at the end in Dürer's final woodcut, as in John's book, all resistance and rebellion against God are overcome. The old gulf between heaven and earth is done away. Righteousness and holy peace are the hallmarks of life in that new city where God and the Lamb reign gloriously under new heavens on God's new earth.

Come, Lord Jesus! *(22:6-21)*

Revelation closes as it opens, with words intended to impress on readers the authority of the Seer and the urgency of heeding his summons to an undivided loyalty to God and Christ. Once more, as in the beginning, John pronounces a blessing on everyone who keeps the words of his prophetic book and again declares that Jesus is coming soon (1:3; 22:7, 20).

Subject Index

Where to Find Certain Key Words and Phrases in Revelation